Praise for Stephan and Nor...

My Father's Keeper

Children of Nazi Leaders —
An Intimate History of Damage and Denial

"A fascinating and paradigmatic representation of the German conundrum: how a post–cold war generation copes with deeds for which it was not responsible, yet whose consequences have left it with a universal guilt. . . . Norbert provided amazing stories of how the families of Nazi criminals fared after the war. Stephan updates us and offers an engagingly thoughtful commentary on the implications of these *Nazikinder*'s survival."

— James Woodall, *Financial Times*

"A powerful book, masterfully conceived, brilliant and devastating. . . . The Leberts have done a remarkable job of breaking a trail through the morass of repression and denial obscuring issues that will continue to disquiet future generations."

— *Publishers Weekly*

"The wide spectrum of responses from these 'Nazi children' — some of whom had Hitler for a godfather — provides the basis for a fascinating and chilling insider account of Germany's violent past and haunted present. . . . Stephan doesn't give any facile answers to the question of how one generation's violence and hatred affects the next. Rather, he allows the psychological mysteries surrounding each of his subjects to resound and deepen. The result is a quietly anguished meditation on the intersection of family dynamics and national history."

— Sandy Asirvatham, *Time Out New York*

"Priests, doctors, psychologists, and psychiatrists report an 'astonishing' absence of psychological problems related to guilt or shame in Germany after the war, and, in many ways, Lebert's study illuminates more general motifs in Germany's collective attempts at 'mastering the past,' a process of judicious forgetting as much as it is one of remembering."

— Tim Kirk, *Times Literary Supplement*

"The younger Lebert has indeed inherited his father's obsessions with matters of generational good and evil. Their shared fascinations have yielded an intriguing, if creepy, revisiting of some of the most horrifying days of the twentieth century." — David Finkle, *Trenton Times*

"An important work, indicating that anti-Semitism is far from dead." — George Cohen, *Booklist*

"An absorbing read, told with sympathy and discretion. All the children have been deeply affected by the loss or imprisonment of their fathers, but in very different ways. . . . Their psychological turmoil seems to be as much about the violent loss of a parent as the legacy of Nazism. To them, these men were their daddies, not the gaunt, fearful men in the dock at Nuremberg. Memory, Lebert concludes, is a complicated business." — Richard Overy, *Mail on Sunday*

"Powerful and poignant; the innocence of little children is contrasted with the evil of their fathers, as the doting parent is revealed to be a human butcher on a scale that still tests the imagination, even as it ices the heart. . . . Riveting portraits of the spawn of evil." — *Kirkus Reviews* (starred review)

"Fascinating reading about family, psychology, politics, and the notion of legacy." — Sandee Brawarsky, *New York Jewish Week*

"The Leberts — meaning, principally, Stephan, since he has the advantage of greater distance — are not out to prescribe how the children of Nazi leaders should feel about their paternity or to chastise their fellow Germans. They instead are engaged in an intricate examination of guilt and denial and repression, all within the parent-child relationship. . . . The Leberts have made a good start at examining, among other things, an uncertainty that should be felt by us all." — Roger K. Miller, *Cleveland Plain Dealer*

My Father's Keeper

Hitler at the christening of Rudolf Hess's son Wolf-Rüdiger in 1938. (Scherl/Süddeutscher Verlag-Bilderdienst)

My Father's Keeper

*Children of Nazi Leaders –
An Intimate History of
Damage and Denial*

by

STEPHAN and NORBERT
LEBERT

Translated by Julian Evans

LITTLE, BROWN AND COMPANY
Boston New York London

First published in Germany by Karl Blessing Verlag as
Du Denn trägst meinen Namen, 2000.
First published in Great Britain by Little, Brown and
Company, 2001
First United States edition, 2001
First Back Bay paperback edition, September 2002

ISBN 0-316-51929-4 (hc) / 0-316-089753 (pb)
LCCN 2001091643

10 9 8 7 6 5 4 3 2 1

Q-FF

Printed in the United States of America

Contents

Prologue

In 1995, the death of an old woman is recorded. The notice in the Deaths column includes the phrase: 'Where Fate begins, the gods end.' You could say that this particular woman had more than one fate. One lay in the fact that for more than forty years she was able to see her husband only on visits to a Kafkaesque prison. For long years he was the sole inmate of this fortress – until the visits ceased, the day he lay dead in his cell. For seven years the woman lived on as a widow, till she also died. Her notice in the Deaths column declared: 'In courage her life ended.'

The preacher at a funeral should have some connection with the life of the deceased. The woman's son telephoned a former minister, a retired religious teacher, and asked him whether he would speak at the funeral service. He added a condition: the man of God should accept only if he could promise that his oration would not come across as too Christian and would, above all, not contain a single bad word about Adolf Hitler.

On the face of it, this is a funeral service like many others. People in black, with solemn, set faces. The mourners each saying a few words. But there is something unusual. The preacher's name is Martin Bormann – junior, the son of the Nazi hangman Martin Bormann. The dead woman's name is Ilse Hess.

Born Ilse Pröhl at the beginning of the twentieth century, at a young age she got to know a skinny boy, Rudolf by name, a boy with the distinguishing characteristic of black circles around his eyes: many attested even then to a brooding, melancholy presence. When Ilse married him in 1931, she could nevertheless hardly have suspected that her husband would turn out to be one of the guiltiest of the Nazi war criminals, a man who even as a lonely, ailing prisoner would make world politics watch and wait with bated breath for decades.

It is important to understand how, living together from day to day, Hitler's inner circle of National Socialists had a sectarian character. Living communally in the Obersalzberg, whenever there was something to celebrate they celebrated together, demonstrating the unfailing strength of their thousand-year friendship. As a consequence of this way of life Martin Bormann junior, the terrible Bormann's son, came to have two very special godparents: on one side Adolf Hitler, on the other Ilse Hess. Thus the question before Frau Hess's funeral was also whether Martin Bormann would speak about his godmother without saying a bad word about his godfather.

Martin Bormann junior, a man who has often lectured in schools on the subject of 'Fascism: Never Again' but who loves his father, delivered the address at the cemetery. He had agreed the text beforehand with Wolf-Rüdiger Hess, the son. 'I wanted to know whether what I was going to say was acceptable. At a funeral, the words need to reach the mourners in their grief.'

The year 1995 – five years after German unity was reattained – was a boom time for the obituaries of another German dictatorship: a series of funerals styled by west German observers as the parting symbol of the collapse of the Deutsche Demokratische Republik (DDR). Only a year earlier, Günter Guillaume had been buried in Berlin – the spy in the chancellor's office who had sparked the fall of Willy Brandt. An open grave, ringed by former top agents, Markus Wolf among them . . . how can journalists fail to be provoked to flights of interpretation by such images?[1]

And what of that other funeral service in Munich: what kind of symbol might be laid bare there? Far from the eye of publicity, Ilse Hess's body had been lowered into the earth to lie with the mortal remains of her husband. Perhaps it was a pity there were no photos of the mourners: they would undoubtedly have become part of contemporary history. Gudrun Himmler, the daughter of the murderer Heinrich, had put in an appearance. Next to her sat Ilsebill Todt, daughter of Fritz Todt.[2] There were many other faces too, well-known names of the time. To

---

[1] Günter Guillaume was a DDR agent. Markus Wolf was the chief of the DDR's secret service.
[2] The Reich minister for armaments who died in an air crash.

whom, one wonders, did they really wish to pay their last respects – only to the dead? Or maybe also, in some small degree, to their own lives? To a particularly unusual and special past?

In his sermon, Martin Bormann picked up on the phrase from the announcement of Ilse Hess's death: 'Where Fate begins, the gods end.' And gently, in his Christian way, repudiated it. No, he said, life never came to an end, it was only a transition to a new time.

He could hardly have put it better, considering the men and women who had come before him to honour the memory of the dead Frau Hess. Because sometimes there are stories – even in an atheistic world – that do not end with the passing of the protagonist.

In the summer of 1999 Martin Bormann, now seventy years old, once again had to deal with the complicated circumstances surrounding funerals. This time as a son, because it had to do with his father, and his father's final remains. At the end of the Second World War the fate of Martin Bormann, war criminal, had been an unsolved riddle. At first he was thought to have disappeared, and, as often around those who vanish, wild theories circulated: he was seen, at least once, in South America in the company of Josef Mengele, the notorious Auschwitz doctor, then in Russia, subsequently in various spots in the Arab world. The most likely theory from the outset, that he had not left Berlin at all but been shot there at the beginning of May 1945 as he attempted to flee, could not for a long time be confirmed, despite the discovery of a skeleton thought to be his. Not until the development of

DNA analysis did it become possible to compare the skeleton's bone tissue with the blood of a Bormann aunt, and for a professor to state, fifty-four years after the war's end, that he was 99.99 per cent certain that the bones were those of Martin Bormann, born in 1902 in southern Germany.

The scientists then had a question. What were they to do with this last small pile of the Nazi's remains? Martin Bormann junior told me that from the outset there was never any question of an ordinary burial. 'We don't want his grave to become another terrible place of pilgrimage for neo-Nazis, like the Hess family grave.' Eventually he applied to have his father's bones cremated. The urn would be buried at sea, in international waters beyond Germany's borders: the exact spot would not be made known.

The burial took place in August 1999. On the day, Martin Bormann and the other Bormann children came together 'to remember in gratitude the father who gave us life', as he put it. Afterwards, when Bormann spoke about it, it was in a distant and detached way. As though it were not particularly important whether his father were alive or dead. His life among the shadows would go on, one way or another.

For You Bear My Name

I'VE KNOWN KARL-OTTO Saur a pretty long time, and pretty well too, as I thought. We met for the first time more than fifteen years ago, when he was teaching at the German Journalists' School in Munich. For several years he was my colleague on the *Süddeutsche Zeitung*, where he was media editor. Karl-Otto is easy to get on with, a friendly, open person, what you'd call a typical '68er, in the good sense. Close-cropped beard, unkempt hair a bit on the long side for his age; his dress sense might strike you as a little out of the ordinary – even when it's not. My feeling about Karl-Otto is that he's a man with a tendency to mockery, occasionally to cynicism; and that he can mostly be relied on to take the right side in politics – the correct side.

I know Karl-Otto's daughter Lela too. I remember when Lela got married and there was a big party in a Bavarian hotel. The whole family was there, obviously: Lela's brothers, her father Karl-Otto and his wife, and his brother Klaus-Gerhard, a well-known publisher. A decent, open family, whose members seemed close and happy together; a family that did not need to put up a front. For example, the fact that Karl-Otto and his wife had had to weather occasional storms and low points in their marriage had never been a secret.

One detail, however, was for a long time unknown to me: that Karl-Otto's own father had had a special past. About this man there is a tale to be told. On the day of Karl-Otto's birth, 14 March 1944, as the Second World War ground towards its end, his father, also Karl-Otto, was as usual at his desk in Berlin, on the executive floor of the Armaments Ministry. Under Fritz Todt, old man Saur had been a leading department head, and after Todt's death in an air crash he rose further, becoming head office principal and *de facto* one of Armaments Minister Albert Speer's two deputies. The first time it strikes the ear, 'Armaments Ministry' does not sound so bad, not as bad as other official names of the period. But bear in mind that Hitler's war machine was kept operational by Speer, Saur and others right up to the last weeks before the war's end, by every available means. In other words, here in the Armaments Ministry the orders were written that sealed the fates of millions of forced labourers. According to historians' estimates, approximately a million foreign workers died from forced labour in the German armaments industry. Burned out, used up: extermination by labour, the Nazis called it.

Karl-Otto Saur was a feared figure, much given to displays of temper, brutal in making sure the job got done.

Industry bosses trembled before him. His outbursts of anger when something didn't go the way he wanted it to were legendary. He can be studied in photographs of the time: he's the broad, thickset man in the Party uniform, often standing close to Adolf Hitler or Albert Speer; the bloke with the bull neck and the razor-cut hair. 'My father', as his son says today, 'gave every outward impression of being the archetypal mean Nazi.' For many years after the war the father had told his children, full of pride, what a good and close relationship he had had with Adolf Hitler. 'I don't know how often he told me that one Christmas Hitler had said goodbye to him in unusually personal terms, calling him "a fine son of Christ".' The father was not exaggerating: Saur's proximity to Hitler is confirmed by various sources. Before Adolf Hitler stuck a pistol in his mouth on 30 April 1945 and pulled the trigger, he composed a kind of mad political testament in the crazy belief that, despite the fires burning throughout Berlin, he would still be in a position to convene the members of a new cabinet. In his hour of death, Hitler named Saur as Speer's successor.

My interest in Karl-Otto Saur senior and his relation to his son came about because of a manuscript that lies in front of me on my desk. It is 148 pages long and somewhat yellowed: even today I can easily picture my father writing these pages forty years ago. I see him like a bird of prey swooping down on its target, stabbing at the keys of his typewriter – he was a journalist and passionate with it, as they say. Up to a few days before his death in the winter of 1993, he was still working, his oxygen flask by his desk. Till shortly before he died we would chat at the hospital about the last piece he was researching: a kind of world history of minor inventors. I sat at his bedside as he died. Shortly before, a thick blizzard had started outside, and I can still remember that the howling wind twice forced open the window in his hospital room.

The yellowing manuscript on my desk, written in 1959, which I only read for the first time in 1999, treats of my father's visits to the children of high-ranking Nazis, the Görings, Himmlers, Hesses and Bormanns of the Party. He showed how things stood with them, fifteen short years after the war's end. His report, laid out over several issues, appeared in the magazine *Zeitbild*. The series was published under the title 'For You Bear My Name'. I was born in 1961, and I remember that the magazine articles were often talked about in the family. Not much about their content, which remained vague. Of all his conversations, my father only spoke about the one with Gudrun Himmler, the daughter of Heinrich Himmler who had so idolised her father. He remembered how long he had needed before this excessively mistrustful girl had decided to place a grain of trust in him. He had felt sorry for her, for the way she had sat in front of him during their conversations, so skinny and transparent-looking. And he always said: 'I could so easily have thrown her to the wolves. But I didn't want to.'

My father's articles played a part in my life for another reason. As a result of the reports, he very nearly went to work for the magazine *Stern* in Hamburg. There was a lot of talk in the business about how my father had been able to get access to the *Nazikinder* (Nazi children) through the interpreter who had translated between Hitler and Mussolini: at the time this was considered quite a scoop, because the children had gone underground. Henri Nannen, the legendary editor-in-chief at *Stern*, wanted the story and invited its author to Hamburg. My father often spoke about the discussion they had. Nannen had been very decent and thoroughly impressive. Particularly impressive were the various interruptions: at one point Nannen was phoned by one of his editors, who swore at him in obscene terms and so loudly that he could be heard across the desk. 'You see' – Nannen grinned at my father, holding the receiver away from his ear – 'that's how my subordinates speak to me.' Shortly afterwards he asked his secretary to pass on a message to another editor, saying that he wished such and such to be dealt with. A few moments later the secretary put her head round the door and said: 'Your editor wants you to know that he won't be dealing with the thing you asked him because he was sacked by you this morning.' 'Bloody hell,' Nannen groaned, 'why does everyone always believe what I say nowadays, when they know I'm so feeble-minded that I never mean it?'

The punchline to the *Stern* anecdote, much cherished and repeated in our family, was that my father was due to fly back to Hamburg to sign his contract: tickets were booked and he was already at the airport when the editor-in-chief of *Weltbild*, a man by the name of Jovy who was also pursuing the material – and the reporter – talked him into having a cup of coffee with him just before his flight left. Jovy must have been a charismatic character: *Weltbild*, he said, was going to become one of the great magazines of Europe, an incredibly rich Swiss publisher was behind the expansion. Somehow this convinced my father, and the plane left without him. He started work for *Weltbild*. It is difficult not to see his decision as an error. *Weltbild* never became a world-class magazine, and closed down less than a year later.

Munich, the late 1990s: Thorsten Schmitz, a colleague on the colour supplement of the *Süddeutsche Zeitung* who was also a friend, mentioned one day that he was doing some research into a tricky subject. There was an organisation, he said, known as *Stille Hilfe*,[3] which supported elderly Nazis: one beneficiary of its work was a Frau Hermine Ryan-Braunsteiner, who had formerly rejoiced in the nickname of Kobyla the Mare because at Majdanek concentration camp she had enjoyed ordering women and children to lie down and then trampling them with her hobnailed riding boots, sometimes to death. *Stille Hilfe* had to be a fairly loathsome organisation, my colleague thought. He knew that a substantial role in it was played by a woman named Gudrun Burwitz, whose own story was creepy enough. Still caring so lovingly for the old perpetrators, she was the daughter of Heinrich Himmler.

Gudrun Himmler. The small, skinny girl my father had felt sorry for. So that was how her life had turned out. At the end of a century that had consigned the project of

[3] 'Silent Aid'.

German National Socialism to Hell, little Gudrun, now an old woman, was looking after her dear daddy's former associates. She was also, it was said, active in the ranks of the NPD;[4] embittered and refusing to see that the world had changed through and through.

Gudrun Himmler. She lived in a terraced house in south Munich. Married to a writer whose name she had taken for her own, and spinning about her a web of cold gloom. There was a daughter from the marriage, a woman obviously long since grown up. When my colleague talked to the daughter, she had become very upset. It would be a catastrophe if her mother got into the papers. None of her acquaintances knew what her mother's name originally was, 'not even my husband knows'.

When I discovered my father's typescript about the Nazi children among other piles of papers in his workroom, it didn't take long for the idea to form: the idea that I would search out these people once more, forty years later, those who were still alive and were willing to meet their former interviewer's son. The result would be something along the lines of a documentary movie, incorporating archive stills from a long-gone time. A journey through time, through a handful of destinies bound to the bloodiest period of German history by a single characteristic: their name.

To Dortmund, where Martin Bormann picks me up at

---

[4] *Nationalistische Partei Deutschlands*, the right-wing German Nationalist Party. A debate is taking place as to whether the party should be banned.

the station. White-haired and friendly, his appearance is very Christian. He has worked for long years as a missionary in Africa. He tells the story of how he had to return because he contracted an acute worm infection. In the Tropical Institute in Hamburg where he was treated, a doctor mentioned to him that not so long before, another man had been admitted also suffering from a worm-related illness, whose name might interest him. It was Wolf-Rüdiger Hess, Rudolf Hess's son, whom my father back then had accompanied on a January day in 1959 when the younger Hess was due at a review to defend his refusal of military service. He could not fight, he said, for a country that kept his father locked up. Today he lives in his terraced house in Munich, firmly convinced that his father was murdered in Spandau.

Thus the paths of Bormann's and Hess's sons had crossed at the end of the 1960s, in an institute for tropical medicine in Hamburg – a clinic with a long and meritorious tradition, but nevertheless with the odd doctor here and there who would have had some contact with the dreadful experiments on human guinea pigs during the Nazi era. Or is that to state matters too sensationally? Perhaps we should put the situation more objectively and soberly: two men fall sick abroad and are treated in a specialist clinic in Germany. What can they do about having the names they have? And what does it mean, anyway, that a hospital has a National Socialist past? Is there a single German institution anywhere without dark stains on the pages of its history?

Back in Munich, the lawyer Klaus von Schirach greets

me with a statistic. Every two years, give or take a few weeks, a journalist from somewhere will try to make contact. 'I can set my clock by them.' The last time it was some newspaper people from Japan who had decided that Nazi children, hey, they'd definitely make a hot subject again! Disgusted, he says of this voyeurism: 'We aren't a subject, or if we are I wouldn't know which.' By 'we' he means, among others, Edda Göring, only daughter of Hermann Göring, about whom my father wrote: 'She has remained the princess Hermann Göring brought her up to be.' Klaus von Schirach says he and Edda see each other regularly and talk to one another a great deal. He is the person who will make contact for me with Edda Göring, who lives an entirely reclusive and somewhat bitter existence in the Lehel district of Munich.

I'm going on a journey into the past that makes me shudder, over and over again. For instance, when Klaus von Schirach tells me about a very old woman who still likes to remember her former boss. Only recently, Schirach says, they spoke to each other again, Frau Junge and he. She was Adolf Hitler's last secretary, and during their last phone conversation she had told Schirach how kind Hitler always was to her, how he liked to give her little gifts, lipstick and make-up. Despite his propaganda chief Goebbels constantly proclaiming that German womanhood should reject all such unnatural adornments. Well, you know, Adolf Hitler was only a man, after all.

There are extraordinary family histories. One can study them to see how fateful family ties can be. You can't help thinking of Shakespeare's tragedies when you sit across a table from a man like Niklas Frank, the son of Hans Frank, Hitler's governor-general in Poland. If those who carried out the inferno of Auschwitz were devils, then Hans Frank was the devil-in-chief. To my father, Niklas Frank came across as an analytical young man who was in the process of facing up to the dreadful truth about his family. Forty years later, in a pizzeria in Hamburg, he speaks to me about the curse of the name of Frank; about the miserable deaths of his brother and sister, and his own despairing hatred.

'I'm sure I've hated my father so very much,' Niklas Frank says, 'because I kept on finding him in myself.'

He laughs when he makes such remarks. A cheerful, infectious laugh. But it sounds wrong, and the discordancy of his laughter seems to intensify the horror. Or is that what is right about it? Niklas Frank: 'The only thing in life that lasts is its grotesque side.'

We know a great deal nowadays about family psychology: what kind of effect it has on a child when its parents divorce, how the fundamental nature of trust is destroyed for good if a child is not properly loved in the first three years, how the unfulfilled wishes of father and mother impose themselves imperceptibly but no less heavily on the children, how the unhappy childhood of one parent is carried over into the next generation. Generally speaking, the understanding of how deep is the stamp of the parent–child relationship is common knowledge in a modern, enlightened world.

It seems all the more remarkable then that one question has still not been fully dealt with. What does it mean for this country called Germany that those responsible for the Third Reich, and their fellow travellers and accomplices, have had children and grandchildren to whom they have handed on their aggressions, their cowardice, their capacity for atrocity, their secrecy and their mechanisms of repression? In most kinds of therapy, the fact that the patient's father had a father who forbade his son's choice of profession has a role to play. Is it not possible that there might be consequences when father or grandfather happen to be murderers?

The *Wehrmacht* exhibition[5] is so loathed by many Germans because it brought out into the open another issue about the Third Reich that had been swept under the carpet: ordinary German soldiery had also been implicated in some of the Second World War's most dreadful crimes. Of course it was hardly likely to have been otherwise; and in reality such a finding, half a century later, ought to be met with little more than a shrug of the shoulders. But for too long – into another millennium – there has been a theory of history doing the rounds, based on silence and a simple formula: there are the bad Nazis, and then there are the other Germans.

There wasn't *the* German soldier, there wasn't *the* German National Socialist, *the* German SS man. There wasn't *the* German fellow traveller and *the* German resistance fighter either. There were perpetrators, first and

---

[5] The first exhibition to document the crimes of the armed forces. Conservative and right-wing parties criticised its suggestion that all German soldiers were criminals.

second class, and maybe third too. Different forms of fellow-travelling existed. One can dispute this as much as one wants, it changes nothing. The collective implication of Germans in the twelve-year-long thousand-year Reich has turned into the legacy of the German people. As have the ways and means by which we deal with it today, and have dealt with it up till now.

When I think of my father, I see him sitting at the dining table, usually with a cigarette in his hand and a cup of coffee in front of him. He was born in 1929, a foster child whose biological father worked in a bar at some racecourse or other, a waiter who one New Year's Eve just had to show a fifteen-year-old girl the inside of his little flat. The thing about the racecourse bar must have a genetic significance, because later on my father was a regular racegoer, as I was later still. There are hereditary factors that you just can't do anything about.

My father was a keen member of the Hitler Youth, even rising to troop leader of a small Munich section: it was a story he often told. At home they had a big map of the world on the kitchen wall, with little flags stuck in it everywhere Germany's soldiers were advancing, at least at the beginning. As a fifteen-year-old living through the collapse of 1945, he had experienced it not as a liberation, he used to say, but as a terrible defeat. He never tried to gloss over this feeling with the excuse that, well, he'd been young then; instead he used to say: 'There is no doubt whatsoever that if the war had turned out another way, I would have got on well in the world with the Nazis. My God, what would I have turned into?' Every time this question stung him to the quick. Every attempt to find out something of what used to bring on this guilt trip of his ended in failure. But perhaps it was why he described the Nazi kids almost gently, without the slightest spite or irony: sometimes his portraits were almost too sympathetic.

This book offers some dramatic destinies: each probably enough on its own for a film or a novel. Careers such as these are closer to us than many of us care to accept. At the mercy of a name, these people – in contrast to many others – had to decide how they would choose to deal with the past. Some, shockingly, chose to follow in their fathers' footsteps.

I often used to turn off the television whenever there was yet another documentary on National Socialism. Yeah, yeah, it was dreadful, I said to myself, but we know it was dreadful. After my conversation with Klaus von Schirach, I stood on the Leopoldstrasse in Munich and suddenly realised how present this history was. The equation 'National Socialism equals Holocaust' had always led me to the point where I thought, oh yes, horror. Horror ticked off like a piece of prep; horror as ritualised as a victim's story on television or at the cinema.

Schirach had spoken to me about the importance of the aesthetic impact of the Hitler Youth, which was created by his own father Baldur von Schirach. And suddenly I'd remembered a photograph, a picture that had recently done the rounds in the German newspapers. It was of a group of young men, beautifully turned out in designer suits: five young writers photographed as they discussed the state of the world, which apparently included their own belief in their position as an elite, a better class. Somehow these five struck me as being utterly typical of their time (possibly because they left such an impression of arrogance and scorn for their fellow human beings). And suddenly I couldn't stop myself wondering whether young men such as these wouldn't have made very effective teenagers in uniform fifty years before. I'm not saying that these are today's Nazis – God forbid. I only wondered whether they might not, back in those days, have been equally well suited to be the embodiment of a ruthless, glacial *Zeitgeist*.

It is details like these that tell you how very much you are stamped by something, the past for example. Late one afternoon, when I was having a conversation with Karl-Otto Saur, we were talking about opportunism. Suddenly it became clear to me why the two of them, he and his brother, both wore their hair too long. I saw the picture of their father: always the clean-shaven neck. The smooth bull neck.

The 1959 Manuscript:

WOLF-RÜDIGER HESS

'Next please!' yells a voice out into the corridor. On the benches in the hallway of the district recruitment office for Munich 1, at number 45 in the Kaulbachstrasse, sit the young men, all born in 1937, awaiting their examination. They smoke, crack jokes, play cards.

Next in line is Wolf-Rüdiger Hess, in slippers and swimming trunks as the regulations require. (In a democracy the examination no longer requires nakedness.)

Wolf-Rüdiger Hess steps forward in swimming trunks and slippers to be examined by the medical commission. Everything's routine. The eye test is satisfactory. Blood pressure and pulse normal.

'Twenty knee-bends, please.'

Heart normal. Lungs likewise. The young man is fit for military service. His service record book will be issued.

The service psychologist is in a room further along. 'Which arm of the service would you prefer?'

'If I didn't find myself obliged to refuse military

service I'd be interested in the mountain troops.'

For a moment it's quiet in the room. The sun throws diagonal beams across the polished floor. Somewhere a phone is ringing.

'Why do you find yourself obliged to refuse military service?' asks the service psychologist.

'My father is in Spandau jail. I am Rudolf Hess's son. Do you understand?'

The service psychologist of the district recruitment office for Munich 1 does not need to understand. He is not responsible for any matters of conscience.

'Write a letter to the objectors' review board, stating your reasons.'

Wolf-Rüdiger Hess gets dressed again, packs away his swimming trunks and slippers in his briefcase, and walks. A few steps away and he finds himself in the English Garden. The lawns are white with daisies and the air smells of linden blossom.

The time is just past two. The next lecture begins at four. Bridge statics with Professor Huber. He still has a couple of hours. He lights a cigarette and strolls through the park: a good-looking young man, tall, dark blond with pale eyes, barely twenty-two.

He stops before a fence. Behind the fence is a small vegetable garden with beds of lettuce, tomato plants, sunflowers. His father has a garden like it in Spandau. He writes often about his garden. 'I've become an expert in the field of tomato-growing this year' or 'This year I'll be concentrating on sunflowers' or 'Now I'm destined for the carrot section . . .'

So the years went by. After carrots, the prisoner of Spandau planted potatoes. A year later, onions. After an interval, son and mother sent him many happy returns for his sixtieth birthday. And, a few weeks ago, for his sixty-fifth.

It is hard for Wolf-Rüdiger Hess to imagine his father. The pictures in the family album are twenty or thirty years old. Against the walls of Spandau photographers make no headway. Only one has so far succeeded in getting beyond the walls and barbed wire with a telephoto lens and conjuring up the shadows of the prisoners. One of them was Rudolf Hess – his father.

The son possesses only his letters, from Britain, Nuremberg, Spandau. Apart from that, nothing, not even a memory. He was only three years old when Hess flew to Scotland. Three-year-olds are not in the habit of forming memories.

Wolf-Rüdiger Hess walks on. He has a couple of bread rolls in his briefcase. (He'll feed them to the swans and ducks on the Kleinhesseloher See later.) He isn't at all hungry today.

He suddenly finds himself thinking about the sunflowers and whether the seeds his father planted have come up. He decides to ask him about them in his next letter. Wolf-Rüdiger Hess has never been to Berlin, nor to Spandau. What would be the point of staring at the walls and watchtowers?

Hess is the only prisoner in Spandau who refuses to receive visitors. 'Under circumstances which I consider to be undignified, I will meet no one in this prison . . .' Today

Wolf-Rüdiger Hess on his first birthday. (Scherl/Süddeutscher Verlag-Bilderdienst)

Wolf-Rüdiger understands this attitude, though as a youngster he could not understand it that day in September 1946, in Nuremberg . . .

He travelled with his mother in an overcrowded train from Hindelang to Nuremberg, changing in Kempten, changing again in Augsburg. There were no seats. They stood crammed in corridors, pressed against each other. A few of the travellers opened newspapers. The trial was on page one in banner headlines, as it had been for months. The boy was able to read and to hear people talking about it.

'Maybe Hess will get off,' someone said.

Rudolf Hess with his infant son. A rare picture of the Führer's melancholy deputy, smiling. (Scherl/Süddeutscher Verlag-Bilderdienst)

'Maybe,' a hoarse voice answered.

'No, they'll lock him up in a madhouse.'

The boy clutched the letter in his pocket. 'Prisoner of War Rudolf Hess, Nuremberg' – the name of the sender. It was addressed only to the boy; he knew every word by heart.

My dear Buz,

I thank you for your letter in which you tell me you've decided you don't want to drive tipper trucks for the postwar cleanup in Munich any more, and instead you're going to be an engine driver for the proper, big railway. I give you my blessing. I understand only too well how much you enjoy speed. Of course you could go even faster as an aeroplane pilot. But probably you've never flown yet and you don't know exactly what it's like. Well, anyway, you've got plenty of time to think about it. I would drop the idea of being a tram driver completely: he's an awful dawdler in comparison with the others, plus he's having to brake all the time because cars, cyclists, people and dogs keep getting in his way . . .

The train leaned into a curve.

'Perhaps the lot of them will finish up with their heads on the block,' said the hoarse voice.

At Nuremberg's main station the boy and his mother climbed down from the train, tired and nervous. Rain dripped through the shattered dome. People lay asleep on the platforms and in the ticket hall.

Mother and son drove into town and found a room for the night somewhere.

The next day Wolf-Rüdiger Hess saw Nuremberg's Palace of Justice for the first time. He walked with his mother down long, endlessly long corridors. Their papers were checked and they were sent from one room to another. New faces all the time. One tall American even shook the boy's hand, but he didn't understand what the man said. Maybe Hess will get off was what the man in the train had said. With his left hand the boy held on tightly to the letter in his pocket. He wanted to go and stand very straight in front of his father and tell him he had thought it over and that he wanted to be a pilot . . .

All the corridors were patrolled by guards, heavily armed and wearing white helmets and white gloves. Some walls were protected by sandbags. Wolf-Rüdiger didn't understand why. He didn't like to ask . . .

An hour later, as they walked through the rain-soaked Nuremberg streets, Wolf-Rüdiger said nothing. He was struggling against tears. The little lawyer who was defending his father had delivered a message to them: 'Herr Hess asks you to understand. He wants to remember his family in happy times . . . Not here with wire screens and guard posts. I'm to pass on his geetings to you . . .'

That was how it had been. That was how it was a few days before the International Military Tribunal sentenced Rudolf Hess to life imprisonment.

Wolf-Rüdiger Hess feeds the last breadcrumbs to the ducks in the Kleinhesseloher See. It is a magical spring day. The waiters in the lakeside restaurant are serving ice-cream sundaes. Chinese lanterns wobble on the rowing boats. Thirteen years before, in the ruins of Nuremberg, no one was thinking about ice-cream sundaes and Chinese lanterns. He had been eight years old and worn a dark-blue suit. Today he's wearing drainpipe trousers and a sports shirt with an open collar; he has no intention of being an engine driver or a pilot . . .

He looks at his wristwatch. It's gone half past three. He should be setting out for the Technical University, but he feels that today he can give bridge statics a miss. I'm Rudolf Hess's son . . . he knows, however, that this is unlikely to suffice for the objectors' review board. He will have to set it all down precisely and thoroughly for them.

Shortly after four p.m. the bell rings in the law office of Dr Alfred Seidl in the Neuhauserstrasse.

'Who shall I say wants to speak to him?' the secretary asks.

'Wolf-Rüdiger Hess. And if you like, you can tell him: Nuremberg.'

He is admitted immediately. Dr Seidl stands behind his desk to greet him. The young Hess towers over him. 'So you're the small boy . . .'

'Yes.'

'Please sit down.' Seidl pushes a bundle of documents aside and inspects the young man before him. When, in 1946, he took on the defence of Rudolf Hess, he was himself a young unknown. Today he is a famous lawyer. He has appeared in hundreds of cases, defended great and small, company directors, pimps, murderers, the innocent and the guilty. But no trial has stayed as fresh in his mind as that of thirteen years before, when twenty-one defendants sat in the neon-lit Nuremberg courtroom, the German Civil Code suspended for the duration, when the accusers wore foreign uniforms, and out of the proceedings rose the ghosts of millions of innocent dead.

'You look very like your mother,' says Seidl. 'Only the eyes, I would say, are your father's. Am I right?'

'Yes.' Wolf-Rüdiger answers with hesitation. Everyone

who has known his father says the same, so it must be true.

'Are you working?'

'No. Still studying. Civil engineering, here at the Technical University.'

'And you're living in Munich?'

'Yes, in lodgings.'

They talk for a short time. Plans, the future. But the lawyer's thoughts are straying into the past. The son's voice and gestures remind him of the father, principal defendant number two, his client. With bowed head and detached expression, he had sat for months next to Hermann Göring. Not one word passed his lips. The other twenty accused had all stepped into the witness stand to testify in their own defence. Only Rudolf Hess had kept silent, until the final day, when he at last declared: 'I regret nothing. If I were starting out again, I would act again as I acted.'

'How is your father?' Dr Seidl enquires.

'Thank you. He manages to bear the loneliness. He's been in prison for nearly twenty years now.'

'And he still refuses to sign the petition for clemency?'

'Yes,' says Wolf-Rüdiger Hess.

Outside in the anteroom there is a clatter of typewriters. The telephone rings. The whisper and clanking of trams comes in through the open window.

'Are you allowed to send him pictures of yourself?' asks Seidl.

'Yes. Pictures are allowed and we've sent him plenty of photographs, but he wrote to my mother that he still doesn't really know what I look like. He says I look different in every picture, depending on the mood or the lighting or the direction I'm looking in . . .'

The lawyer nods. 'What can I do for you?' he finally asks.

'I was called up today,' says Wolf-Rüdiger Hess. 'Fit, obviously, but I want to refuse military service. As long as my father stays in Spandau, I will not be a soldier. So now I have to give the review board precise reasons. In order to do that, I need to know the grounds for judgment against my father.'

Seidl presses a button. 'The Hess file, immediately, please. And I'm not to be interrupted.'

The same evening Wolf-Rüdiger Hess sits in his rooms in Bogenhausen and writes a long letter to the conscientious objectors' review board. The letter is dated 8 June 1959.

I am happy to set out for you the detailed circumstances behind my father's detention in Spandau . . . On 30 September/1 October 1946, before the International Military Tribunal, my father was found not guilty of war crimes (count three of his indictment) and crimes against humanity (count four). On counts one and two – preparation of a war of aggression – he was found guilty and sentenced to life imprisonment . . .

In the judgment in my father's case attention is drawn to his having provided sustained and active support to preparations for war. To bear out this view the court refers to the fact that my father was signatory to the law of 16 March 1935 implementing compulsory military service . . .

The tribunal of that time was composed, with the exception of the USSR, exclusively of members of the present NATO alliance – an alliance to which, as we know, the German armed forces are affiliated. You will undoubtedly appreciate that my conscience today forbids me from performing military service for those who were my father's judges.

This letter, filed at the district recruitment office for Munich 1 (under file number PA-110/59/IV/37), was the opening shot in the Wolf-Rüdiger Hess case: a case that would make its way through several courts and create a considerable sensation on the way.

In the 1930s the Hess villa was to be found on Munich's Harthauserstrasse, up by the bank of the river Isar, with park, swimming pool and tennis courts nearby. It was here that Wolf-Rüdiger came into the world, on 18 November 1937. Hitler was his godfather.

The day that changed the life of the Hess family completely was 10 May 1941. Rudolf had been at home for a few days. At noon he received Alfred Rosenberg[1] and spoke with him behind closed doors for about an hour. Then he retired to his study.

[1]   Reich minister for the occupied eastern territories.

At about half past two he emerged to speak to his wife. He was dressed in an unusual get-up: blue-grey breeches, a blue shirt and high aviator's boots.

'What's the matter?' Ilse Hess wondered.

'I've been called back. Unfortunately the holidays are over. I have to go to Berlin immediately.'

'When will you be back?'

'I don't know yet . . .'

Hess went to the nursery, but young Wolf-Rüdiger was asleep. A few minutes later Ilse Hess heard the whine of the Mercedes' supercharger.

Two evenings later Hess's youngest aide burst into the house with the news: Hess's plane had gone down over the North Sea and he was presumed dead. Ilse Hess placed a priority call to the Obersalzberg, but Hitler did not come to the phone. Instead *Reichsleiter* Martin Bormann eventually spoke to her. 'We don't yet know anything for certain,' he told her.

Only on 13 May did it appear in the newspapers that the Führer's deputy had jumped out of a Messerschmitt Me-110 'in a state of mental confusion' – the Nazi press knew how to phrase these things. Orderlies, aides, secretaries, chauffeurs and friends of Hess's were nevertheless arrested.

Ilse Hess, leaving Munich with her small son, moved out to the Bürgle, to a pretty summer house in the market town of Hindelang in the Allgäu. The villa in the Harthauserstrasse was left empty.

'We had two ponies in the Bürgle,' Wolf-Rüdiger Hess remembers of this time. 'My grandmother and my aunt lived with us. Apart from that –' he shrugs his shoulders, 'the only thing I remember is my first day at school.'

'What about news of your father?'

'A few letters reached us through the International Red Cross. The first one took eight months. There wasn't much in it because of course in Britain my father had to feign amnesia.'

'Herr Hess, you know that for a long time it has been put about that your father really did lose his memory and his reason.'

'I could prove the contrary to you a hundred times over,' the young Hess replies. 'But my father's already taken care of it. He didn't want to find himself in any way described as unfit to stand trial at Nuremberg. That was why he made an official declaration to the court that he had feigned memory loss in Britain for tactical reasons.'

'Was his declaration sufficient?'

'It was good enough, because my father showed he could still remember all the questions the British psychiatrists had asked him. He even knew the wrong answers he had given them. And the right ones, obviously.'

'What was his real reason for adopting that tactic?'

'In his farewell letter my father advised Hitler simply to declare that he was insane if his mission to Britain backfired.'

Wolf-Rüdiger is interested in his father's mission only in the context of what happened to his father. 'I'm not concerned with any other political questions. That goes for the present as well as the past.'

In the spring days of May 1945, when French and

Hitler at the Hess home in the spring of 1939. (Bayerische
Staatsbibliothek Bildarchiv)

Moroccan troops occupied the Allgäu, the son of the
Führer's deputy was in the third year at the *Volksschule*. A
French captain interrogated his mother and had the house
searched for classified documents. Apart from that, nothing happened. They scraped by, grandmother, aunt,
mother and son. Like millions of other Germans, no
better and no worse. In Hindelang Wolf-Rüdiger Hess
was only known as Buz, and the farmers' and tradesmen's
sons he shared his school bench with weren't bothered

that he was the son of a senior Nazi. Buz played a tearing game of football and skied like a pro: in Hindelang this was more than enough. By the end of the war most of the children had no father at home: German fathers were languishing in hospitals and prisoner-of-war camps, fallen, missing in action.

Wolf-Rüdiger's father was brought from Britain to Nuremberg in late autumn 1945. They read about it in the paper. The first letter didn't arrive until January 1946: 'Don't be taken in by bad flash photographs or any slanted reports you may read. I have changed neither inwardly nor outwardly. Naturally I have lost a little weight: I deliberately eat less than before because I feel so much fitter . . .'

Buz sends a letter every week to his father in prison in Nuremberg. The talk is of beating other teams at football, of dogs and cats, school, the swimming pool, childish concerns and anxieties.

'We must expect the worst when it comes to the sentence: death, prison, secure hospital . . .' the Führer's deputy writes to his wife on 2 September.

On 1 October they sit before the radio in Hindelang and listen in silence to the summing up. 'Hess was Hitler's closest personal confidant . . . the leading personality in the Nazi Party . . . supported Hitler's policy of energetic rearmament . . . a willing participant in Germany's aggression in Austria, Czechoslovakia and Poland . . .'

Next day at school, during break, one of Wolf-Rüdiger's classmates says, 'Your dad's alive, that's the main thing. Are you coming to singing this afternoon?'

He shakes his head. 'Not today.' Not a thing more is said among the nine-year-olds.

Eventually the Hess family had to leave the Bürgle. They moved temporarily to the Gasthof Hirsch until a couple of rooms became available in a farmhouse in Bad Oberdorf. Ilse Hess sold her jewellery. Buz started at Hindelang secondary school.

On 3 June 1947 a police sergeant knocked at the door.

'I have to ask you to come with me, Frau Hess,' he says.

'To come with you – am I to take it that you're arresting me?'

'Something like that,' the sergeant grunted. 'In any case it will be best if you pack your toothbrush.'

'Why am I being arrested?' Ilse Hess asked.

'It's at the request of the Bavarian Ministry for Special Affairs.'

Ilse Hess took off her apron, packed a few belongings into a small case, and patted her son on the shoulder. 'It can't upset us, can it, Buz?'

'No,' said Wolf-Rüdiger.

He ran to the hayloft and watched through the opening under the eaves as his mother walked away with the policeman.

Would she get life too?

Ilse Hess was taken first to a prison at Sonthofen, then on 6 June she was brought to Göggingen labour and internment camp near Augsburg. She moved into hut V, room 5.

The camp at Göggingen was separated into a women's

and men's camp. Huts, barbed wire, watchtowers . . . It was a camp where there would soon be children playing, children with names like Hess, Göring, Frank, Schirach. Many of them encountered each other for the first time here, and most of them never saw each other again. The Göggingen camp was the last common thread in their destinies.

Who Were the Fathers?

For his escape he gave himself a new name: Heinrich Hitzinger, sergeant. In the end it was probably better to be a small man, one among many. As part of the disguise he shaved off his moustache and covered his left eye with a black eyepatch. And the deception might have worked; he might have remained undiscovered for a long time. When he was picked up on 22 May 1945 by a British patrol in the Hamburg area, together with a number of his followers, at first it occurred to no one to doubt the authenticity of his identity card. He looked emaciated enough, and he was hardly a figure of dread any longer. His band had been on the march for ten days through a ruined Germany. And where were they going exactly?

The British soldiers brought him along with the others to camp 031 near Bramstedt. It is a reasonable guess that it didn't suit him to be dealt with the way he was, as a supposed sergeant. As a figure of high rank he was, naturally, used to things being different, to being surrounded by secretary, driver, bodyguards. It is well known how hard it can be for some to relinquish the reins of ordinary power. How much harder to give up the despot's power? Perhaps it is not surprising that after only one day of internment he requested a meeting with the camp authorities. He had something to tell them, he said: as indeed he did. He entered the room, removed his eyepatch and said: 'My name is Heinrich Himmler.' Quite possibly he had imagined that as a more important perpetrator, he could count on better treatment.

The truth was that a countdown had started that would last only a few hours longer. Himmler was straightaway ordered to remove his clothes; an ampoule of potassium cyanide was found in his jacket. He was given a British uniform to wear and locked up. Shortly afterwards, we know the following exchange took place between the examining doctor and a Colonel Murphy.

'Did you look in his mouth as well?' asked Murphy. When the doctor answered in the negative, Himmler was fetched from his cell. 'Open your mouth.' On hearing the words, Himmler bit together: he had had a potassium cyanide capsule in his mouth all along – enjoying the feeling of playing with it, letting his tongue roam over it and stroking it for hours, possibly days. For twelve minutes the British fought to save the life of one of the greatest mass murderers in history. They stitched his tongue down and inserted a tube into his stomach, with the intention of pumping out the poison. Twelve minutes later he was dead.

Let us imagine the few years of National Socialism as a

source of material for writers and film directors. What a treasure chest! If there were ever to be a lexicon of humanity's abysses, most of the period's leading figures would have a place in it. In reality one needs scant art from the artist to fashion the characters; all that is necessary is to retell the biographies once again. Everything can be found there: not just the madness and atrocity, but everything down to the confusion of contradictions and ideals, of disturbed mental states and the longing for a kind of beauty and total power. All of it contained neatly within the themes of rise and fall, megalomania and violent death. As for the score, one need supply only one musical suggestion: the operas of Richard Wagner that were the only music heard in the last days of the Führer's bunker in Berlin. Even the music reflects the monstrosity of the subject: the Führer's clique was utterly, almost joyfully aware of its own drama.

Goebbels, for instance, a few days before he and his wife committed suicide – Magda Goebbels already having poisoned their six children Helmut, Holde, Heide, Hedda, Hilde and Helga – held a last staff meeting in which he again played the devil. Formally dressed, in dark suit with sparkling white shirt, he swore at the German people for their cowardice, then, calming down, became cool and ironic. 'But after all,' he said quietly, 'the German people chose this fate for themselves. Nobody forced them into it. It appointed us of its own free will. Why did you work with me? You're going to lose your heads now.' Then he limped to the door, turned round once more and said: 'But the whole world will tremble at our going.'

It is strange how distant such stories are. Of course the historians have investigated every corner of the Third Reich, but sometimes it seems as though, in all the noting and appreciation of the facts, no one really wanted to know anything at all of the human interest behind the perpetrators' stories. We know that for a long time this was true of the victims' stories. Only when the American television series *Holocaust* – at first so sneered at – was broadcast in Germany did the wall of silence break down.

The perpetrators. As though they had been swallowed up by the mist of horror that was sprayed collectively over the dark years. No one wanted to look back, to know whether the dark shapes did not perhaps display the odd characteristic that would be familiar to us all. There was a general feeling that the best way to exorcise the ghosts was to try to lock them up for ever in a kind of scientific-historical horror movie.

The author and journalist Maxim Biller has said that as a Jew he is occasionally reproached for the characters in his stories and for his point of view as a journalist, for their being stamped time and time again by the wretched past, by the traces of the Holocaust. Maybe so, he has responded, maybe the shadows have played too great a role in his work. He has posed a counter-question: What does it mean, then, that among young non-Jewish German writers, the German past and traces of Nazi dominion never, or highly infrequently, surface in their texts and words?

In this book we speak of children, children who have

been unable to rid themselves of the images of their fathers. To understand their situation, we must look again with our own eyes at the kinds of images that keep them captive.

Heinrich Himmler was born on 7 October 1900. Reports from his schooldays say he was a good, quiet pupil. One of his fellow pupils would later testify: 'He could not hurt a fly.' Another said: 'Heinrich was a little lamb.' He was not a sportsman and was unable to take part in the students' club drinking bouts because of a nervous stomach. He was teased at length as a result.

This is one image: a gentle nature, vegetarian (a breakfast tip: leeks and mineral water), keen supporter of animal rights. He loved herb gardens and throughout his life hated it whenever anyone told a dirty joke about women in his presence. He had a certain taste for the occult; he was very interested in the existence and possible effect of earth rays. No one who knew him has failed to attest to his qualities as a good and loving husband and father. He always made time for his daughter Gudrun, they say.

Heinrich Himmler was chief of the SS, the *Reichsführer-SS*. He built the SS into what it was: a personal army, an elite unit separate from the military and police. The best of the best: you could not get more Nazi. Specialists in 'brown special operations' of every kind; which means also specialists in murder and mass murder. It was Heinrich Himmler who on 4 October 1943 in Posen delivered to an assembly of *SS-Gruppenführer* the following speech, which has become branded on the German soul:

> It is fundamentally wrong for us to try to carry our naturally innocent nature, our good nature, our idealism, to foreign peoples. That goes for Herder to start with, and his 'Voices of the Peoples' that he scribbled down in a drunken hour and which has brought us, his descendants, such boundless pain and misery with it. It goes for the Czechs and Slovenes too, whose national feeling did not exist before we brought them to it. They themselves were incapable of it and we had to discover it for them.
>
> One principle must be absolute for the SS man. We are to be honest, decent, loyal and good comrades to those of our own blood and to no one else. How things stand with the Russians, how things stand with the Czechs, is of no interest to me whatsoever. What exists by way of good blood of our kind among other peoples, we will take for ourselves, stealing their children if necessary and bringing them up among us. Whether other peoples live in prosperity or whether they perish from hunger interests me only in so far as we need them as slaves for our own culture, otherwise it does not interest me in the least. Whether during the construction of an anti-tank ditch 10,000 Russian women collapse from exhaustion or not interests me only in so far as the anti-tank ditch is finished for Germany. We will never be brutal or heartless

where we do not need to be; that is clear. We Germans, who are the only people in the world to have a decent attitude towards the animal kingdom, will hold a similarly decent attitude to such human animals, but it is a crime against our own blood to concern ourselves with their fate or bring ideals to them . . .

I want to mention to you here in all openness another, difficult subject. Between ourselves it is to be said out loud once, in a perfectly open manner, and thereafter we will never more speak of it in public . . . I am speaking now of the evacuation of the Jews, the eradication of the Jewish people. It's a subject people tend to talk about very easily – 'The Jewish people is to be eradicated,' says this or that Party member, 'of course it is, it's there in our programme, elimination of the Jews, eradication, let's do it.' And then they all come, those decent 80 million Germans, and every one has his good Jew. Of course they know the others are swine, but this one is a first-rate Jew. Among those who talk that way, not one has witnessed the actual thing, not one has seen it through. Most of you will know what it means for a hundred corpses to be laid out in front of you, for five hundred to be lying there or a thousand. To have seen that through to the end and – apart from exceptions due to human weakness – to have behaved correctly is what has made us hard. This is an unwritten and never to be written page of glory in our history . . .

That is the other image: Heinrich Himmler, deviser of the system of the concentration camps, who with the same automatism of the perfectionist dealt with that most murderous of all tasks. Towards Hitler he demonstrated a submissiveness that was nothing short of doglike. He did and would have done everything his Führer demanded of him. All his life, he tried to satisfy Hitler's wishes, often before he had formulated them himself.

Yet Himmler was more than just a man who obeyed orders, ready for every task. Hannah Arendt talked about the 'banality of evil' in connection with Adolf Eichmann, a close colleague of Himmler's. Himmler had nothing banal about him. As though he had grown to be driven by hatred of his own weak side, he dreamed of perfect human beings. He was the man who brought the *Aktion Lebensborn* programme into existence, a breeding institute for Aryan women chosen for their blondeness and good looks. He had already had part of France set aside for himself and his idea: there, in Burgundy, he was to have created 'a paradise of the German race'.

The journalist Joachim Fest said of Himmler in his brilliant book *The Face of the Third Reich* that he was 'a romantically overwrought petty bourgeois who, under the conditions of a dictatorship, was granted the power bloodily to live out his inclinations'. Fest further stated that such a man would only have had his chance in a society which was itself utterly deranged.

One more image: a crazy petty bourgeois, who ordered the most appalling medical experiments on human beings in the concentration camps – and simultaneously ordered the planting of herb gardens. Possibly the two things were, in his brain, somehow the same thing.

Martin Bormann was forty-five when the war ended, when he died. He was the archetypal man who wants only one thing in life: power. His qualifications were ideal: he was brutal, ambitious, determined to prevail, mistrustful and scheming. Had he been lucky enough to grow up in the second half of the twentieth century rather than the first, his career path would presumably have been at least as steep, though possibly slightly calmer in character.

Hitler's secretary – that was his official title. He himself once said to his wife, long before the end of the thousand-year Reich, that if she ever found herself arranging his funeral she was not under any circumstances to preserve his orders and medals; it would let a false impression grow of 'what I have really achieved'. He saw himself as the string-puller behind Hitler, exercising more influence on policy than anyone else. A view in which he was clearly right. At Nuremberg he was condemned to death in absentia for his substantial participation in all Nazi war crimes, from the persecution of the Jews to the conduct of the war.

The image of Martin Bormann is crowded with photographs. In group portraits he keeps himself mostly in the background, in others he can often be seen at Hitler's side, a stout man with his head close to his Führer's ear. Martin Bormann will remain in our memory as the dark, amorphous shadow of National Socialism. Even though his son, christened Martin like his father, intended a different meaning to the title of his autobiography, it sounds remarkably appropriate: *Living Against the Shadow*.

No one could bear Bormann. 'Everyone hated him,' said his fellow Party member Hans Frank, 'and the word "hate" is not enough.' Bormann snooped, had his comrades spied on, used his insider knowledge in intrigues of every kind. Others among the Nazi myrmidons had at least one secretary or official who protected them; Bormann had only enemies. Not just in his public life – there are few kind accounts of the private man. He used his power to collect lovers, and kept his wife informed in cheerful letters whenever he made a new sexual conquest. He should just be careful, she once wrote back to him, that he didn't get his lover and her pregnant at the same time, so that he would always have a 'fully fit woman' at his disposal.

Baldur von Schirach can be seen as the baby of the Nazi heroes. His relationship with Hitler began when he was a student. Of good family and just twenty years old, he persuaded Hitler that he must extend his movement into the universities. At first Hitler was sceptical, mainly on account of his loathing of things intellectual, but as more and more students attended and applauded his speeches, his contact with von Schirach became closer. When the young man later married the daughter of Hitler's personal photographer, a man called Hoffmann, the couple were presented with a German shepherd dog as a wedding present.

At the beginning of the 1930s Baldur von Schirach was responsible for coordinating all youth organisations and for turning the Hitler Youth into a compulsory programme. It was von Schirach who translated Hitler's fanatical concept of youth into reality. The National Socialist dictatorship was, among other things, a dictatorship of youth, of beauty and energy. National Socialism gave to young people the feeling that tomorrow belonged to them alone – so much so that it was even worth dying for.

Like Himmler, he was the antithesis of the ideal that he preached. Flabby in stature and bearing, with a weakness for the arts (he wrote grandiloquent poems to his Führer), he was anything but a man's man. In reality he was an introverted, melancholy eccentric who discovered early on that he possessed a profound death-wish. He was the seducer who brought hundreds of thousands of young people to calamity; later, he liked to portray himself as the suffering victim who had himself been seduced. At the Nuremberg war-crimes trial he said he had only one thing to mention in his defence: he had believed in Hitler, he had believed that this man would 'make our children happy'.

After serving a twenty-year prison sentence, he was collected from Berlin-Spandau by his children: he was half-blind, a broken man. He had become the NSDAP's[1] youth leader at twenty-four. He died at the age of sixty-

---

[1] The *Nationalsozialistische Deutsche Arbeiter Partei* or National Socialist German Worker's Party: the Nazi Party.

seven. On his gravestone is the inscription: 'I was one of you.'

Hans Frank was, as Joachim Fest writes, one of the most contradictory phenomena in the National Socialist leadership. On the one hand weak, soft-hearted, uncertain, on the other attracted by the brutal and barbarous, he decided early on that as far as he was concerned every means was justifiable to implement the National Socialist ideology. His decision was to become reality.

Hans Frank was, in turn, Bavarian justice minister, head of the legal office of the NSDAP, and then governor-general of Poland with special responsibility for mass murder. When he was arrested by the Americans he would try to commit suicide by slitting his wrists, but he could not bring himself to cut deep enough. He would hand over to the Americans art treasures worth several million dollars which he had had confiscated from the dying, plus his thirty-eight-volume diary. Speechless, the Americans would study his precise accounting. Conversations with Hitler he would note down along the lines of 'My Führer, I inform you that today I have exterminated another 150,000 Poles . . .'

In the months before he was hanged, Hans Frank discovered the Roman Catholic faith and endeavoured by that path to escape his guilt. In a conversation with a prison doctor he remarked: 'I am two people, the weak Frank and the other, the Nazi. And one is always asking the other: What have you done?'

As the legacy of Hans Frank to future generations I

offer two quotations, a diary entry for 16 December 1941 and an extract from his closing speech at the Nuremberg trial, remarked on at the time by observers as being particularly untruthful.

On 16 December 1941:

The Jews are also injurious to us by reason of being extraordinary gluttons. We have in the governorgeneral's territory roughly 2.5, possibly, with those who are closely related and all their dependants, 3.5 million Jews. These 3.5 million Jews we can neither shoot nor poison, but we will nevertheless be able to take specific steps which will, in some manner, lead us to an exterminative success . . . Where and how this will happen is a matter for responsible bodies that we will and must set up here and of whose effectiveness I shall notify you as promptly as I can.

Closing speech in Nuremberg:

At the beginning of our journey we never imagined that our turning away from God could have such corrupting, fatal consequences and that we would inevitably be ensnared ever more deeply by guilt. We could not know then that so much faith and self-sacrifice by the German people could be so abused in our care. And so in our turning away from God we came to grief and had to perish. It was not through technical shortages and bad luck alone that we lost the war. Nor was it by disaster and betrayal. God, above all, has delivered judgment on Hitler and carried it out upon him and the system which we served with god-forsaking energy . . .

Hermann Göring enjoyed saying things like this about himself: 'I am what I have always been, the last Renaissance man.' He was always one for the grand pose. 'I was the only one in Hitler's circle who had his own authority.' This was true. He had returned from the First World War as a highly decorated fighter pilot. What pushed him into the arms of the Nazis, early on, was not their ideology but their idea of struggle, 'the struggle itself was my ideology'. Hitler valued in Göring the fact that 'It can't be done' was not in his vocabulary. 'Whenever I talk to Göring it's like a spa bath for me, every time.'

This is one picture: the brutal fighter who stepped over the corpses of others, and with other like qualities played a highly influential role in the time up to the seizure of power. Once during this time when he came to a meeting with the British ambassador Sir Eric Phipps, explaining his slight lateness by the fact that he had come straight from hunting, the Englishman answered coolly: 'Animals, I trust.'

The other side of Göring was the prototype of the power politician who, after a very short time on the throne, loses his grip on any kind of reality. He piled up titles, collected more decorations. He feathered his nest relentlessly and at home was happiest playing with his pet lions. He put on weight and became seriously addicted to morphine. The one-time war hero emerged as a sick man playing the hero. When his only daughter, Edda, was born, it came as a considerable surprise to the nation, since Göring was believed to be sterile as the result of a war wound, and the German people allowed themselves a joke: *'Sein oder nich sein, das ist die Frage.'*[2]

Hermann Göring was condemned to death at Nuremberg: he had been the driving force behind the war of aggression and the author of the campaign of oppression against the Jews. The night before he was to be hanged, he poisoned himself.

Rudolf Hess was without doubt the darkest and most obscure of the leading Nazis. A gloomy, ravaged character, he came to life only through his boundless admiration for Adolf Hitler. 'I love the thought', he used to say, 'of being putty in someone else's hands.'

It looked for a long time as though the Hess marriage would be childless. So badly did the Hesses want a child that they sought help from innumerable miracle cures. Finally it happened: little Wolf-Rüdiger was born and his father danced for joy, as the saying goes. Poor Wolf-Rüdiger: his father's case was to become a lifelong task for him.

At his birth every *Gauleiter* was instructed to send to the Führer's deputy a small sack full of German earth

---

[2] This joke is untranslatable, relying on two meanings of the German word *sein*, the verb 'to be' and the possessive pronoun 'his'. Thus the lines 'To be or not to be' from *Hamlet* can also mean in German 'His or not his, that is the question'.

from each *Gau*, or district. The earth was spread beneath a specially prepared cradle so that the infant would symbolically begin his life on the whole of German soil.

Hess, like Hitler, sat in the Landsberg prison after the abortive putsch in 1923, and he collaborated in the composition of *Mein Kampf*. He was Hitler's deputy, delivered the Christmas address every year, and was thought of early on as a scatterbrain and a worryguts who lived in constant fear of his food being poisoned. Everything about him was a puzzle: the curious flight to Scotland in 1941, his internment, his behaviour at his trial at Nuremberg, and finally his death in Spandau in 1987 after more than forty years' incarceration, the last twenty years as the sole inmate of that great prison.

The 1959 Manuscript:

WOLF-RÜDIGER HESS AND THE NAZI WOMEN

'WHAT'S THE camp like?'

'Completely bug-infested.' The guards grinned and led the Nazi women – 'the prominent wives of Nazi chiefs', in the Allies' description – through the camp gates.

Ilse Hess was not the only one to have her first encounter with bedbugs on this occasion. In Bavaria, on 3 June 1947, the wives of all Nazi leaders who had been sentenced or executed at Nuremberg were arrested. The arrests were announced that morning by Special Minister Alfred Loritz at a press conference in Munich.

The American photojournalist Daniel de Luce did not wait for the end of the press conference. He jumped into his Chevrolet and sped to the Jachenau, where Henriette von Schirach, wife of the Hitler Youth leader sentenced to twenty years in prison, and her four children were living in a small country hotel. 'Nazi wives before their arrest': it would be a juicy subject for the US papers.

'I'd like to take a few pictures of you,' he said, unpacking his camera. 'Where are the children?'

'They're catching frogs in the Jachen,' Frau Schirach answered, then, suspicions aroused, she asked: 'Why do you want to take pictures?'

'You're going to be arrested today,' the American calmly explained, 'and sent to some camp. You should get yourselves over to the British zone, because the arrest order's only for Bavaria.'

Daniel de Luce photographed the shocked woman, drank a cup of coffee and drove happily back to Munich with his exclusive.

An hour later Henriette von Schirach was arrested on her way into the village. She tore herself away and tried to escape across a field. The policeman caught up with her and said, 'Be reasonable, Frau von Schirach.'

But she was not reasonable. She clawed and spat and had to be dragged to the car by her hair. Her four children, Robert, Richard, Klaus and Angelika, to whom she had not been able to get word, stayed behind.

Her first stop was a prison at Tölz. In her cell she came upon Luise Funk, whose husband had also been given a twenty-year sentence. The wife of the former Reich minister for the economy wore a checked dirndl and had earth on her hands: she had been arrested while working in her garden.

'It's good that we're together, at least,' said Luise Funk.

Brigitte Frank, wife of the executed governor-general of Poland, had been fetched from her kitchen. The village policeman of Neuhaus-am-Tegernsee had arrived rather self-consciously. 'Frau Frank, I have just had incredible news . . .' He coughed nervously.

'What is it?'

'I must arrest you.'

'Now?'

'Yes.'

'It was one of the very few occasions', remembered Niklas Frank, eight years old at the time, 'when my mother cried. She certainly wasn't crying for herself, but we were five children and there was very little money in the house.'

Niklas went to the railway station with his mother – another whose arrival was awaited at the Göggingen camp, near Augsburg . . .

Emmy Göring was arrested in a forester's house at Sackdillingen in Franken. She was lying in bed with sciatica and had herself certified by two doctors as unfit to travel. Her lawyer lodged an appeal against her arrest.

The appeal was refused. Emmy Göring was fetched by ambulance. She took with her a nightdress and a black coat by Balmain, the Paris fashion house where she had once shopped.

Little Edda, seven years old, asked her as she was taken away: 'Can the denazification tribunal sentence you to death too?'

'No, they can't, definitely not.'

Emmy Göring was carried into Göggingen on a stretcher.

Now they were together. Camp life began.

The five long huts of Göggingen camp – a former

labour camp for female foreign workers – housed approximately a thousand women: girl members of the Hitler Youth, concentration camp supervisors, the wives of SS men hanged at Dachau and Mauthausen, prostitutes and those denounced by their neighbours. Only a barbed-wire fence separated them from a large men's camp in which soldiers of the Afrika Korps, civil-service undersecretaries, bank managers, officers and drunkards awaited their release.

'There were love stories, real betrothals with the men on the other side of the barbed wire, exchanges of rings through the fence,' Henriette von Schirach wrote of this time. 'There was a nurse who loved a doctor in the men's camp. She had a chance to see him in the mornings when they took the urine samples from the sick bay over for analysis in the bigger clinic in the men's camp. But there weren't enough urine samples, so the camp guards were tricked with camomile tea each day. There were men who cut the fence with wire cutters so that they could embrace their girl, men who spent the whole day locked in a cupboard because there was no possibility of getting back to their own camp.'

There were also, at Göggingen, 'interned babies'. They slept in empty soapboxes and each day a pail of milk was delivered for them. In June 1947 there were eight of them. Their number increased month by month, some learning to walk, others newborn; the children of chance affairs behind barbed wire. Ugly, pale-faced, undernourished infants, who never knew their fathers.

Each day the guards collected some of the women and

girls for interrogation. These interrogations were important. They might hold the key to an internee's freedom.

Judith, one of the Hitler Youth girls, got out in the space of a single interrogation. She spent hours on her make-up and getting ready. Long black eyelashes, lipstick, bra of gold-coloured lace, tight sweater – every resource mobilised. She looked terrific as she walked out.

When she returned to the hut after her interrogation, she packed her stuff together and announced: 'I've had enough of the rats here. I want a bathtub, I want to eat, I want to live. Look after yourselves, girls!'

She moved into the villa of the camp superintendent – a Mr Strauss. The camp staff were soon able to admire her elegant nightgowns. But not for long. She quickly tired of Mr Strauss, and while he was away on a business trip she brought in a removal company, loaded up the villa's furniture and a batch of tinned food for good measure, provided her identity papers with the necessary stamps and disappeared.

Mr Strauss was transferred, and a thousand women laughed. There was not a great deal else to laugh about . . .

Whenever the public-address system was switched on, the prisoners fell silent and listened anxiously to the announcements. 'At Landsberg today the executions took place of *SS-Gruppenführer* Wegener, *SS-Obersturmführer* Wieland, *SS-Oberscharführer* . . .' It was not uncommon to see a desperate wife throw herself onto her straw mattress in a flood of tears, having heard the announcement of her husband's death.

The wives of the 'prominent Nazi chiefs' remained in their own way prominent at Göggingen. But it brought them no advantages; they were as subject as others to the snap roll-calls in the middle of the night, the sirens howling and the clank of floodlights. 'Everyone outside!' the sentry would order, and the women would be forced to parade in ranks in their nightdresses. Inspected and leered at, they were a ridiculous sight, and the camp personnel made the most of it.

'Emmy!'

Frau Göring stepped forward. She was already in trouble with the camp superintendent for putting up a picture of Hermann again the minute after she had been ordered to take it down.

'I've been lucky,' wrote Ilse Hess to her husband after Nuremberg,

> since I've apparently got the friendliest hut out of all those that are available. We're under the orders of our hut senior. She is small and delicate but has a deep, man's voice, smokes like a chimney . . . My special favourite is a very worldly-wise old lady from Munich with a good sense of humour; sixty-three, knows Harlaching and once cleaned your offices in the Brown House . . . I don't let myself think about the boy, though thinking about the little lad is always a terrible temptation . . .

When Wolf-Rüdiger first visited his mother in Göggingen, the regulations were harsh. 'I was led into a visitors' room. My mother sat at the end of a long table. I was permitted to sit at the other end of the table and we were allowed to talk to each other for about half an hour in the presence of the soldiers on duty. Then I went back to Hindelang with my aunt.' To this visitors' room came the other children, one after another: Edda Göring, Norman Frank, Robert von Schirach . . . Time after time the same worried questions were put: How are things at home? Are you getting enough to eat? How's school?

On 18 July, a hot summer's day, the PA boomed into the brooding midday heat: 'The seven prisoners and leading war criminals Hess, Raeder, Funk, Neurath, Dönitz, Speer and Schirach have today been taken by air from Nuremberg to the Spandau fortress in Berlin.'

Suddenly in the afternoon the Nuremberg prison chaplain, a man named Achtermann, appeared in the women's camp. 'The departure came as a great surprise,' he reported. 'The Americans are sticking to the Potsdam Treaty. The prisoners must be kept under four-power control. We packed blankets and a pullover for each in the plane . . .'

'This is the first letter from the new quarters,' wrote Rudolf Hess on 3 August.

Fundamentally it does not differ from the old. On the less agreeable side, there's the fact that we may only write a letter of this length once every twenty-eight days. We're allowed to receive one letter in the same period. To the positive side of this new existence belongs the fact that the rooms are newly painted

and therefore cleaner. And imagine: I have a pil-
low, with a pillowcase, a white-linen-covered
mattress . . .'

Life behind bars becomes a habit – in Spandau or
Göggingen . . .

At Göggingen camp life acquired a less harsh, more
balanced rhythm. Of late the authorities had begun
broadcasting music over the PA and sermons on Sundays.

Showers were installed. Growing spinach was allowed
in narrow beds, and a black market got going: you could
trade coffee, chocolate, face cream, cigarettes. But there
were no signs of release.

Ilse Hess eventually filed an application with the camp
superintendent to be allowed to have her ten-year-old son
with her in the camp for a few weeks.

The application was granted, and the young Hess
moved in. He slept on a camp bed next to his mother. The
camp wasn't bad, he thought; at least it was better than
school.

The case of the Hess boy got talked about.

After Wolf-Rüdiger, little Edda Göring arrived, blonde
with blue eyes and a round forehead. The spitting image
of her father . . .

Edda Göring brought a full knapsack with her into the
camp. As Emmy Göring unpacked it, the women in the
hut waited expectantly. Possibly a packet of coffee would
appear. Or a sausage. Or at least some face cream . . .

But the knapsack contained only a dark-yellow teddy
bear and four different outfits for him.

Edda ran on her long skinny legs through the camp. She curtseyed prettily and could recite a poem by Adelbert von Chamisso. Before long there would be postcards of her for sale in every German newsagent's and stationer's, portraits of her hanging in prams and parks.

Wolf-Rüdiger, almost identical in age, had time for neither teddy bears nor poetry. Each day he slipped past the barbed wire into the men's camp to while away his time there. Among the watchtowers, huts and latrines he found something to appeal to his boyish sense of romance. He could try on battered pith helmets, go rat-hunting, collect old tin cans and listen to wild stories. In the evenings when, tired, he crawled back to his mother's hut, he wrote enthusiastic letters to Spandau.

'So you want to learn chess too,' his father wrote back.

Very good. I had it taught me when I was twelve, along with Uncle Alfred, who was a year younger then than you are now. We both had scarlet fever and couldn't be with other children for a long time . . . As I got older I became so good that when I was a soldier in hospital at St Quentin during the First World War and there was a chess champion from Berlin called Cohn who played us in twelve games of chess simultaneously, I was the only one who beat him.

Yesterday evening I thought about you a great deal. I've got a picture of you in my mind as a big and growing boy. And next to yours I saw some other pictures; one of them was of Mummy's face with the same fair hair as yours. A few days ago it was twenty years since we got married – how time races away with us . . .

The letter was dated 25 December 1947. 'Yesterday evening' would have been Christmas Eve. In Spandau prison Walter Funk played Christmas carols on a harmonium for his fellow prisoners. In Göggingen internment camp the huts glimmered with the candles on small, scrawny Christmas trees. And elsewhere on this Christmas Eve of 1947 there remained hundreds of thousands of others behind barbed wire somewhere in Russia, in Siberia, the Urals, the shattered soldiers of a lost war. Did they have any idea it was Christmas?

On 23 March 1948, after a hearing of the denazification tribunal, Ilse Hess was released from Göggingen camp. The house in Harlaching had, as a matter of course, been expropriated and all other assets were lost. Ilse Hess began to build herself and Wolf-Rüdiger a simple existence in Bad Oberdorf.

Wolf-Rüdiger joined the Hindelang Football Club and won his first downhill skiing races, but the academic reports he brought home were miserable.

'I gather from your letter, dear Buz,' wrote Rudolf Hess on 28 August 1949,

that you're well on the way to becoming a football star. That 'brilliant left cross' is obviously the sign of great things to come. But I hope I can rely on you to discover over time that your leg- and footwork needs to be completed with some brainwork. And since, while we are talking about that brainwork, you have had it confirmed in your report that there is plenty of aptitude there and you could achieve more if you exerted yourself more, I obviously don't need to have any worries on that score, do I . . . I can't think you have any intention of alarming me! Whenever the pleasures of laziness try to hold you back in your schoolwork, think of what I'm expecting of you. In short: show that you're beginning to become a little man.

Ilse Hess stuck this letter up with drawing pins over her son's desk. What Rudolf Hess had written to her on the subject was carefully concealed:

Don't have too many school worries about Buz. After everything I've heard reported about the lad in the past few years, it doesn't seem to me that his disposition gives the slightest cause for alarm. All in all, I feel I must agree with Speer, who told me he thought we were dreadfully irresponsible fathers. When one of his brood brought home a very good report, he wrote to her that the one thing she should avoid, for heaven's sake, was to become a model pupil – her marks in her next report were sensational . . . The girl's mother found suitable words to retaliate against the father's child-rearing techniques . . .

In 1951 Ilse Hess rented a farmhouse on the Gailenberg near Hindelang and opened a boarding house there. Wolf-Rüdiger started at a boarding school at the foot of the Hohe Göll, an hour away from Berchtesgaden; it was a combination of secondary school and technical college. Every boy at the school had to decide on a craft. Hess chose the joinery workshop.

Every month he had a letter from Spandau with the same return address: Allied Military Prison, Prisoner of War Rudolf Hess. None of his fellow pupils cared. None asked him any questions. It was a kind of unspoken agreement. When there were twelve letters bundled up in the drawer, another year had gone. Those twelve letters

The end of the road: the prison at Berlin-Spandau.
(Bayerische Staatsbibliothek Bildarchiv)

had to say as much as they could, enough for three hundred and sixty-five days . . .

The young Hess received the benefit of his father's child-rearing skills by correspondence course.

'You tell me you've received my long letter, the one directed exclusively to you,' he wrote on one occasion.

Out of interest I looked at my earlier one again; I noticed I had written down no fewer than eight questions, out of which you answered only two properly. So I suggest you read my last letter again thoroughly before you reply. Even when there are no questions asked in a letter, it's an important part of good manners in letter-writing to show interest in whatever's on the other person's mind. 'Best best wishes' don't quite make up for what's missing, however much I treasure them from you . . .

And on the subject of grammar: 'Are you aware of the difference between "apparently" and "ostensibly"? The majority of Germans use them interchangeably. I'll explain it to you . . .'

In 1953 the boarding school in Berchtesgaden erupted in scandal when two masters were arrested for homosexual activities. Ilse Hess fetched her sixteen-year-old son home as quickly as she could. Wolf-Rüdiger would go to Salem. But the castle school at Salem declined politely and firmly. 'The Margrave Berthold von Baden cannot see his way to admitting the son of the former deputy of the Führer to his distinguished school.'

So Wolf-Rüdiger returned to Berchtesgaden. His boarding school was now called the Christophorus School and belonged to the Christian Youth Village Fellowship.

One day he would not forget was 26 April 1955. A filthy day, with fog covering the mountains and lying thick in the valley of Berchtesgaden.

A thin, unpleasant rain was falling. The two young men negotiating the steep, narrow cross-country paths down to Berchtesgaden were nevertheless in a good mood. Dressed in waterproof capes and walking boots, they looked like woodcutters.

'How much cash do you have on you?' asked Wolf-Rüdiger.

'Three marks. What about you?' Heinz Hartmann answered.

'One fifty.'

'That'll do,' grinned Hartmann. 'Four glasses of wine, cigarettes – comes to four marks forty altogether. We'll have ten pfennigs over.'

'What if the waitress brings us saltsticks?'

'She can always try,' said Hartmann.

The pair had a Latin period behind them and a dancing lesson ahead of them. Beneath their rain capes they wore their best suits with ties and white shirts.

After the dancing lesson they planned to go to the Café Fischer with Karin and Sigrid. For four marks forty, with ten pfennigs in reserve.

Berchtesgaden's first houses appeared through the mist. They came to a road and walked faster.

'Does Karin still go to school?' asked Hartmann.

'Yes. Heydeneck High School or somewhere. Her father's apparently a furniture manufacturer. Anyway, she's already asked me if I have any connection with Hess Furniture.'

They both laughed.

In an alley opposite the Königsee station they changed their shoes and rolled up their rain capes.

'Dead on time,' said the young Hess glancing at the station clock.

They turned into a side street. With only about another hundred metres to go, Hartmann saw a soggy newspaper hanging on the kiosk wall. He stopped, shocked.

'What's up?' asked Wolf-Rüdiger.

'Your father,' replied Hartmann softly and pointed to the paper rack.

The headline was in red. Rudolf Hess had made a suicide attempt. Beneath there were black letters that became too blurred for the young Hess to read.

He tore the newspaper from the rack and skimmed the announcement: 'As Associated Press has learned from Spandau, the former deputy of the Führer, condemned to life imprisonment, yesterday attempted to take his own life by swallowing insecticide . . . The prisoner is seriously ill but his life is no longer thought to be in danger . . .'

While he was reading, Hartmann had bought the evening papers. 'It's the same in all of them,' he said.

For a long moment Wolf-Rüdiger said nothing. 'Bye, Heinz,' he said finally.

'Where are you going?'

'Back to school to talk to my mother on the telephone.'

'Don't be stupid.'

'I have to.'

Forgetting to change back into their walking boots, they ran back the way they had come in their polished town shoes. Hartmann had difficulty keeping up with his friend. Nothing was said between them.

Hess telephoned from his housemaster's room. The minutes while he waited for the connection to Hindelang were endless. Ilse Hess's first words were: 'I don't believe it, Buz.'

'What don't you believe?'

'The attempted suicide. Perhaps it was just an accident . . .'

'An accident with insect powder?'

The line crackled. Otherwise it was quiet. 'Shall I come home?' Buz asked.

'No. I've warned your father's lawyer, Herr Seidl. I'll call you as soon as he has anything to tell us.'

'Shouldn't I still come home?'

'No. Goodnight, Buz.'

The young Hess went back to his room. Hartmann stood at the window and stared out at the foggy night. He turned round when he heard the doors.

They lit themselves cigarettes.

'I'm always thinking about that American doctor, Vancil,' said Wolf-Rüdiger softly. 'After his visit to Spandau, reporters asked him what his impressions had been. "I'd rather be dead than live here," he said . . .'

'And what does your father say?'

'Nothing at all. He never complains. His letters to me are always as though he's just away somewhere on holiday, do you know what I mean?'

That night the two friends sat on the bed, smoking and talking about fathers. They conjured up faces they no longer knew. They picked through their memories like two old men. Heinz Hartmann's father had been killed at Monte Cassino when his son was seven years old.

Two days later the Spandau prison authorities denied the claim that Hess had attempted to take his own life, though the denial offered no further explanation. 'Is he ill?' reporters insisted.

'No comment.'

Roughly a week later, Associated Press reported that Rudolf Hess had begun a hunger strike.

It was a month before Wolf-Rüdiger had another letter from his father:

It sounds to me as though you've all fallen for one of those newspaper hoaxes. There is no question of me 'giving up the race'. It's true that for a little while my health wasn't as good as it might have been. I had no appetite and I was eating very little and losing weight. Recently I've been eating with a much more healthy appetite and putting on weight again. You can set your mind at ease . . .

Wolf-Rüdiger passed his journeyman's examination in joinery, won the Chiemgau skiing championship and took his *Abitur* exams in the summer of 1956. In the same

Wolf-Rüdiger Hess aged twenty-three, wearing a ceremonial helmet. By this time he had won his fight not to serve in the German Army. (Hulton Getty)

year he enrolled at Munich's Technical University to study civil engineering, and to earn money he studied part-time and worked as a theatrical extra, news boy and supply teacher. 'Next year,' he would say, 'I'm going to Sweden to work as a lumberjack.'

So far, so normal. It wasn't till the student refused to serve in the armed forces that he found himself centre-stage. The spotlights all turned on him: the son of Rudolf Hess, Rudolf Hess's son . . .

Twice that year Wolf-Rüdiger Hess came before the

conscientious objectors' review board, the first time on 23 February at the district recruitment office, the second on 19 July at the regional recruitment office. The first hearing lasted half an hour, the second an hour. Twice the young Hess attempted to clarify his conflict of conscience to the judges.

'My father has been condemned because in 1936 he, with others, helped to create the German *Wehrmacht*. For that reason he remains in the custody of the Americans, British, French and Russians today. I am now supposed to report for duty in a new *Wehrmacht*, required and maintained by the Americans, British and French . . . You will appreciate that I am unable . . .

'I refuse military service neither for religious nor ideological reasons,' Wolf-Rüdiger stressed at both hearings. 'I would withdraw my application immediately if my father were to be released from prison.'

The adjournment to consider judgment lasted five minutes at the district office and twenty at the regional office. The outcome was identical. 'The conscript is not entitled to refuse armed service. As a result of the order to report at the recruitment office he is available for basic military service. Place and time of his entry into service will be made known through his call-up order.'

The second judgment acknowledged that his application was understandable in the circumstances of the father–son relationship and that it testified to his strong sense of family, but could not be sanctioned in law. 'It is the view of the board that the conscript is not subject to an imperative moral constraint.'

Thus the son of principal defendant number two at the Nuremberg trial found that he would be compelled in the near future to don military uniform. Except that, at the eleventh hour, he decided to appeal to Munich's administrative court and file suit against the German Federal Republic.

On a Home Page the Story Continues

HE STILL HAD so many questions for his father. It would have been his greatest wish to be able to ask those questions. It was as though his father was an oracle to be questioned, practically an omniscient god who sweeps away all doubt. For no one could more passionately love, respect and admire a dead father than he does. Whatever Rudolf Hess said and wrote during his lifetime was Wolf-Rüdiger Hess's bible. And how much he would still have had to say, says the despairing son, 'what a great German tragedy, that the spring ran dry before it was allowed to flow'.

Rudolf Hess died at Spandau in 1987, in the Allied military prison. The deputy of the Führer was ninety-three years old. Officially the cause of death was suicide by hanging. His son, however, is convinced that his beloved father, around whom his whole life has revolved, was killed. He speaks of proof, of hard evidence. But no one wants to hear – yet another reason why today Wolf-

Rüdiger Hess looks at the world so bitterly and filled with hate.

His questions. What did you talk to Hitler about the last time you spoke privately, before you flew to Scotland in 1941, before your 'peace flight'? What exactly did the Führer know, what did you arrange between you? 'I'm sure', Wolf-Rüdiger says, 'Hitler knew about the flight down to the last detail. Their last conversation is supposed to have been loud and heated. At the end Hitler said to him, "Hess, you are and always were a pigheaded bastard."' He, the son, becomes animated as he tells the story, as though he is thinking: Wow, my father and the great Führer!

He would liked to ask too what his father and Alfred Rosenberg had talked about on that last day. But naturally the son's curiosity would not centre only on the flight to Scotland. He would like to have had some account of the early years of the National Socialist movement, of its beginnings. It must have been a phenomenal time, those first years, fascinating, he says, 'simply unparalleled'. He had for a long time tried to persuade his mother to put her memories of those early years on tape, 'I even bought her a tape machine specially, but she wouldn't. A few times she said something into the machine, but each time she erased the whole thing. Why I don't know. She never liked to talk about the time before. Now she's dead. Now it's too late.'

We're sitting in a Bavarian restaurant outside Munich, in the suburb of Gräfelfing. Wolf-Rüdiger Hess takes his time over the menu, though 'I already know what I want.

I always look through the menu, and then I have roast pork.' The waitress arrives. He orders roast pork. To look at him you wouldn't guess the state of his health: he's an imposing figure, with a high forehead and hairline and a ruddy face – your first impression might be of a rather jovial, eccentric character, to which he will add that he has had a thoroughly enjoyable and jolly life. Has he had, does he still have, friendships that have nothing to do with what happened to his father? Yes, he says, obviously, the friends he plays cards with, his sporting companions, that kind of people – 'I've never talked about my father with them.' Yet it is clear that his commitment to his father takes up most of his free time. In an interview a few years ago he said: 'I never had any free time, I spent all my free time on my father.'

Hess is a dialysis patient: his kidneys are shot, as they have been for a long time, for the last nine years. Three times a week he goes for treatment. It lasts for six hours, with him lying in an out-patient cubicle 'with television, headphones, everything'. Afterwards you're completely exhausted, washed out, he says, 'once or twice at the end of a dialysis I've collapsed, I was so shattered. The best you can do is go home and go straight to bed. You can't do much more.' He is on the waiting list for a kidney transplant, but there are too many terminally ill patients on the list and too few donor organs. 'Maybe it will all work out one day,' I say. His answer is pessimistic: 'It doesn't look very promising.' He remarks that the medical world earns a great deal of money from dialysis, too much to make it really want to change the system. His mistrustfulness is evident when he talks about this.

On one of his many African journeys in the 1960s and 1970s he caught a dangerous parasitic disease. He had to go several times to the Hamburg Institute for Tropical Medicine; each time the treatment lasted weeks. His theory is that the powerful doses of medication he received eventually damaged his kidneys.

Wolf-Rüdiger says that his period in South Africa was one of the milestones in his life. Not because of his illness, but because it was there he experienced for the first time the difference between the truth as described with one voice by the media, and the real truth. What did he mean? Well, he says, everywhere you went people were entirely agreed on how dreadful this regime of apartheid was, with its oppression of the black population. We only touch on this subject, but the couple of sentences he says about it can be roughly summed up as follows: racial segregation is the only solution, obviously under the leadership of the whites, who else? We delve no deeper into the subject.

For a long time it looked as though our meeting would not come about. In reply to my first letter, Wolf-Rüdiger told me that because of his impaired health and his consequently restricted schedule, he was able to receive only selected visitors. I should therefore write and tell him exactly what I wished to know from him. Then he would decide whether this project would be interesting for him. By the way, he could no longer remember meeting my father forty years before.

It is no easy matter to compose a couple of lines so that someone you absolutely want to meet will, so to speak, bite. My point of view is, if you like, that of a voyeur. So I wrote to him that I was interested in his theory of how his father died, in how families stayed together through hard times; something along those lines. He replied in a couple of dusty lines that none of it interested him, I should read his books. Sorry.

My next try a few weeks later was to write that I'd appreciate the chance to talk to him about National Socialism in general: how, according to him, the revision of the past had turned out, how his own summing-up would go. Fairly rapidly, a fax came back. OK, stubbornness he appreciated; I could come.

He fetched me a couple of days later from the S-Bahn station in a bulky blue Mercedes. The story as my father had written it had ended in 1959. Today was a beautiful March day in the year 2000. How had those forty-one years between gone for him? How had his story continued?

Wolf-Rüdiger had finished his engineering studies with the highest grades. He joined a successful engineering consultancy that was run by a man with a past, a man who had been on Albert Speer's staff. Wolf-Rüdiger made a career for himself, quickly rising to a respectable salary. For several years he worked as a consultant on building projects in various Arab countries. He was able to afford a big Mercedes, a house in a smart Munich suburb. His best work, he says, was the development of a new international airport in Hamburg. He had had a hundred people and more working under him as the coordinator. In the end, for political reasons, the airport wasn't built. A shame, he says, adding that now he supposes there'll be a giant airport built at Berlin-Schönefeld. He'd find that an interesting challenge, his experience could be very useful: maybe he'll offer his services. As he says it, it sounds as though he means it. Maybe with a new kidney. Maybe he can still do something there.

The matter of his military service came to a favourable conclusion. In 1964 Wolf-Rüdiger Hess was finally recognised as a conscientious objector. One may, I think, proceed on the assumption that things were not quite as they seemed, because obviously his justification – the imprisonment of his father – could not be accepted as a reason for refusing to serve. Had things gone according to the letter of the law, it was perfectly possible that the son might also have ended up in prison. He would definitely, it seems, have been ready to go to jail for his father. But at some point during the proceedings there had been someone in a position of authority who did not care for headlines in the papers and, of all the cases under his jurisdiction, wanted particularly to see the back of this one.

In 1969 Wolf-Rüdiger had visited his father for the first time. Their first meeting was very emotional but also deeply awkward. It had taken place in a visitors' room, four metres square with a table in the middle at which his old father was sitting – by then he was seventy-five. 'We had the situation under control,' says Wolf-Rüdiger, 'our family has always had a strong sense of self-discipline.'

There had been 102 visits in total, right up to his father's death. He had kept accurate accounts, noting every visit; he could also claim back his travelling expenses from the Free Rudolf Hess Relief Association, a group that had set itself up to campaign for the release of Hitler's deputy. This organisation, which counted many old soldiers among its members, had paid for the journeys to Berlin, to the prison at Spandau. Most of the time Wolf-Rüdiger had travelled to see his father alone: his mother had accompanied him on about thirty occasions.

In 102 visits, he was never alone with him. Usually one of the prison governors was present, a Russian, a Frenchman, an American or a Briton. (The prison remained under four-power Allied control and responsibility.) The conversations between father and son were handicapped by the regulations: no talk of politics, of National Socialism, of the time before. If either party overstepped the line, the interview was immediately terminated. All physical contact, even a handshake, was forbidden. Five minutes before the end of the visit a warder would begin to count out loud. Did he still dream about this situation sometimes, about these visits? No, said Wolf-Rüdiger, or then again maybe he did, but in the morning he never knew what he'd dreamed, 'every time it all disappears'.

Wolf-Rüdiger Hess says that for many years he had only one preoccupation: his father's release. For that reason too he kept out of political discussion, he didn't want to risk getting drawn in and ending up in some authority's bad books. He led a very circumspect existence. Never once expressed his views about National Socialism. Today, now that he knows that all his attempts and hopes were in vain, there is no such caution. Today he speaks his rage loud and clear. Indeed, one of the reasons for his anger is the question: was it a mistake to have always been so well behaved and reasonable?

He solicited support from all quarters, had personal meetings everywhere. With chancellors, whether Willy Brandt, Helmut Schmidt or Helmut Kohl. With the federal presidents Scheel, Carstens, von Weizsäcker. All helped, or at least went through the motions. Each year they would plead again for clemency at the Allied Council. The old man who had once been Rudolf Hess could surely be released, at long last, from his ghostly oubliette? But none of it was to any avail, not even when Hess's lawyer Alfred Seidl embarked on a political career, rising to become Bavarian justice minister, and tried every means in his power to alter the situation. Hess turned eighty, eighty-five, ninety, but the Allies remained unbending. As though in some way they wished to use him, to immure him as a living memorial. As though these four great nations wanted perpetually to replay the story through this stooped old man, so that people would not forget quite so quickly what Germany had done to this world.

As the years went by, another notion took hold in the son's head: they won't let my father out because they can't bear the truth, the truth my father would tell. About National Socialism, about Hitler, about the extermination of the Jews, about his flight to Scotland in 1941, about the Allies' own war guilt. Such was to become Wolf-Rüdiger

Hess's personal version of the story: the hero in prison, while outside lay the collective forces of untruth. One day, he says, this factory of lies will collapse and people will recognise that National Socialism was something quite different from the regime of terror it was alleged to be. And as he eats his roast pork, this seriously ill man says that one day the German people will no longer put up with all the lies that are spread about Germany's history. And clearly the moral greatness of his father will, one day, appear in the history books as well: Rudolf Hess, martyr to peace, as his son likes to call him. Who flew to Scotland in 1941 to salvage world peace, to impede the course of the war . . .

The death of the ninety-three-year-old prisoner fits naturally into the son's perception of these matters; one merely has to work a bit to get the facts straight. The Soviets under Gorbachev had signalled their consent to a possible release – therefore the British needed to get rid of his father so that he wouldn't be able to say anything uncomfortable about Churchill and the rest of them. There are admittedly a number of unexplained circumstances surrounding Hess's death, inconsistencies like those that emerged with the Stuttgart-Stammheim terrorist suicides.[1] Wolf-Rüdiger commissioned a report by an

---

[1] On the same night in October 1977 that the hostages on board a hijacked Lufthansa airliner were freed at Mogadishu, Somalia, the leaders of the Red Army Faction, Andreas Baader and Gudrun Ensslin, killed themselves in prison, though the circumstances were never revealed.

independent expert that casts some doubt on the official cause of death. There are contradictory witness statements. Whatever really happened, it is clear that Wolf-Rüdiger won't be budged from his murder theory by anything on earth. Niklas Frank, son of the butcher of Poland, Hans Frank, has said he has always been glad his father was hanged. At least he had that. The idea that his father might have gone on living all those years, as Hess did, would have been seriously hard for him to bear: he believes that 'from that point of view things were harder for Hess's son than for me. If you look at it that way, his fate is heavier than mine.'

A March day in the year 2000, somewhere not far from Munich. Thus Wolf-Rüdiger's story unfolded, the story of a man who had grown into an ardent admirer of Hitler. One of those who doubted that the organised Holocaust had ever happened. An anti-Semite who maintained that if a people were persecuted over a long time, there must be a reason for it. If, in his words, a child is rejected by his classmates at his first school, it may be the class's fault. But if the same thing happens at the next school, and again at the third, 'then it's the child's fault. And it's exactly the same with the Jews. Of course there are other kinds of Jews too, I don't deny it, my father had very good relations with individual Jews.' Hess senior's ideas have been adopted by his son down to the last comma. The result is an ailing, embittered, immovable man who even now denies the scale of the Holocaust.

I remain silent for long periods during our conversation. I reflect on how my father might have behaved, sitting opposite this man. Would he have kept silent as I did, or would he have become angry, faced with this . . . this old Nazi? Angry because he was thinking: How can you? How can you admit that all you've gained, the only conviction you've drawn from this entire appalling story is that everything was, in fact, quite different, that everything was wonderful? Would he have asked him how he was able to reconcile his views with the photographs from the camps, the pictures of mountains of corpses? The pictures of the emaciated and starving? The fates of those who had been exterminated simply because they were Jews, simply because men like his father had declared them to be a variety of vermin? Had none of this history dismayed him? Would my father have said to him in anger, though anger was futile: Is that all you can do, to show a little charity for a single life, no other acknowledgment than that all the others lied and only my father, the great Rudolf Hess, and I . . .?

Or would my father have been sad more than anything else? Was there in the young man he encountered then an inkling of the old man of today, yet with none of it really foreseeable? Might my father have had a pang of sympathy for him then? For one whose external circumstances had made it all too easy to cast his life into dark places, into persecution mania and incoherent, wildly selective special pleading? What would become of any of us if we knew our fathers only from 102 grotesque meetings spaced out over twenty years, in the constant presence of prison staff?

I remember a photo, one of the pictures reproduced in one of Wolf-Rüdiger Hess's books: the young Wolf-Rüdiger, perhaps three years old, looking up at his father standing, hands folded, a few feet away. But the decisive element in the picture is the man who is rubbing the boy's chubby cheeks. It is Adolf Hitler, in uniform. The Führer is evidently speaking to the little boy, and I think to myself: What was said? And then: What kind of chance did the lad standing between these two men actually have? What would he have had to do to turn out differently from the way he turned out? It is the first time during these visits to the Nazi children that I have asked myself this question. It won't be the last.

I hear myself in the Bavarian restaurant asking Wolf-Rüdiger how he feels about his father being an idol of the neo-Nazi scene. Terrible, he replies, it's terrible. He must have been invited a thousand times to their meetings? 'I've never been. Of course they would celebrate me, but these people are too simple, too stupid, too primitive. I have absolutely no interest in such people.' On the contrary, he says, they damage the whole thing, including his father's memory. 'They think we're still in the 1930s. They have absolutely no concept that we have to go further, to think in the context of the times we live in.'

What then did he think of a man like Jörg Haider, the Austrian popular right-winger? 'He', says Wolf-Rüdiger, 'is a man of a certain calibre, someone I approve of. A modern politician, who has something to say.' He observes Haider with great interest: a man he would almost certainly vote for, were he in Germany.

A final question: Have there ever been moments in his life when he has felt his father's name to be a curse? 'A curse?' he answers immediately. 'No, not once, never.' He doesn't understand the question. How could the great name of Hess be a curse? You know, he says, he has always had terrific support for his work on his father's behalf from ordinary people, ordinary Germans. The books have sold well, they were mini-bestsellers. 'My father's name is still well received. My father was popular with the people, even today that hasn't changed. I've never been personally rejected on that score, on the contrary.' It would be truer to say that Hess's name has been useful to him.

He talks about his own son, who is already a young man, as he was himself forty years ago. He too is interested in his grandfather, in his fate. His name is Wolf Andreas. In his book about Rudolf Hess, *No Regrets*, Wolf-Rüdiger writes of sending news of the births of his three children to his father in prison. The first daughter was born on 23 April, and Hess senior sent back his best wishes in a letter, gently mocking the 'accuracy of your aim', an allusion to 20 April, the Führer's birthday. In an unlikely coincidence, when a year later little Wolf Andreas made his appearance, all fitted into place. His date of birth was precisely 20 April.

The father today waxes enthusiastic about his son. 'He has grasped entirely the significance of his grandfather's life.' The son is a computer freak, the father says proudly, and is setting up his own home page for Rudolf Hess. 'It's an amazing thing.'

The story is not yet done.

The 1959 Manuscript:

MARTIN BORMANN JUNIOR

BENEATH THE IMAGE of the Madonna of Maria Kirchtal burn twelve candles.

The bride and bridegroom stand in front of the altar.

'I ask the bridegroom,' the minister begins solemnly, 'have you examined your conscience before God, and have you come here of your own free will to enter into holy matrimony with this woman, your bride?'

'Yes.'

It is quiet in the little pilgrims' church. One or two women reach surreptitiously for their handkerchiefs. The pews creak softly.

'Are you ready to love your future spouse, to honour her and keep yourself only unto her, till death you do part?'

'Yes.'

It is the third marriage celebrated on this day, 13 August 1960, high above the Loferertal in the baroque church of Maria Kirchtal. A marriage like thousands of others. A bride in white, with white roses, tears and the sound of the organ and a male voice choir.

Nothing unusual strikes the few passers-by who happen to be visiting the church. They glance at the backs of the bride and bridegroom and leave without knowing what kind of wedding party this is, kneeling in the pews in their Sunday best with their gold-embossed prayer books. Without noticing that the minister and the bridegroom are the spitting image of each other.

The minister now stands close to the bridegroom. The church walls send back his words like an echo. 'Are you ready to receive the children whom God may be pleased to send you, and to bring them up according to your duty as a Christian father?'

For the third time the priest, garbed in white, has formally addressed the groom, and for the third time the young man in his black suit answers yes.

They are two brothers who are speaking. The priest's name is Martin Bormann, the bridegroom's Gerhard Bormann.

Their mother has been dead fifteen years. Their father too disappeared fifteen years ago: *Reichsleiter* Martin Bormann, the most powerful man after Hitler, sentenced to death *in absentia* at Nuremberg, sought by intelligence services all over the world and not yet found . . .

In the pilgrims' church of Maria Kirchtal the bride and groom kneel. The young Martin Bormann reads the Mass.

The bells ring out.

Bormann is not the priest at Maria Kirchtal. He belongs to the Order of the Heart of Jesus Mission and is a senior master at the monastery school of Salzburg-Liefering. Gerhard Bormann works as an electrician at Freising near Munich. The family celebrations will take place later in Essen because there are two more brothers and a sister who live in the Ruhr.

It is not by chance that they have sought out this remote Austrian pilgrims' church for the wedding, however. For the eldest son of the infamous *Reichsleiter*, Maria Kirchtal was once a fateful place.

On 15 April 1945 the National Socialist educational establishment of Matrei in the Tyrol closed its doors. Fourteen texts by Adolf Hitler were taken down from the walls and about fifty boys were sent home.

One of the fifty was Martin Bormann. The day before he had celebrated his fifteenth birthday. Today he was dressed in the brown shirt of the Hitler Youth, complete with buckle, shoulder straps and sheath-knife, on his way to Munich. A spotty adolescent who at Matrei had been taught above all how to decline the phrase 'final victory'.

In Munich he searched among the ruins for his father's headquarters. He found them in the process of being closed down. A secretary named Hummel took the boy on one side. 'Your father's in Berlin. We have no news of him. The best thing you can do is see if you can get through to your mother's.'

'Where is my mother?' asked the lad.

Hummel took him to the wall map. 'This is Wolkenstein, and this small place is called Gröden. Your mother's living there with your sisters. It won't be easy to get through. I'm not receiving the regional summaries any

The Führer's godson in the uniform of the National Socialist school at Matrei in the Tyrol. (Hulton Getty)

more, but we think most of the area's already in enemy hands.'

The young Bormann hitchhiked as far as Salzburg. The city was packed with troops from every arm of the services. Salzburg was the dead end, the place where the German retreat had come to a full stop. The Russians were coming in from south and east, the Americans from west and north. The situation was worse than hopeless. Despite the chaos, scattered soldiers were still being collected together and formed into new units. Orders were still being given, and the *Gauleiter* was still at his post.

Martin went to see him. The *Gauleiter* looked at the boy for a while in silence, then said something that surprised him.

'You must take off that uniform and change your name. I'll have some false papers made out for you immediately.'

'Why do I have to change my name?'

'Why? Because Bormann is not such a good name to have any more.'

'Where am I to go?'

This question the *Gauleiter* could not answer. 'Don't worry, you'll scrape through somehow. If anyone picks you up, just remember to keep quiet about your father. The best thing would be to say that you lost your parents in a bombing raid in Munich.'

Martin left the *Gauleiter*'s office wearing borrowed civilian clothes and with false identity papers in his pocket. He found somewhere to sleep in an army barracks and attached himself to a regrouped SS unit. When the last order came through, the fifteen-year-old was in the ranks with the others. The order was: 'Defend the Alpine fortress.' Unfortunately none of the soldiers knew the fortress's whereabouts. The SS troops pulled back into the Lofer mountains. In the high valleys above Weissbach and St Martin they fought on until 5 May. On that day they either gave themselves up or donned civilian clothes and attempted to disappear.

The young Bormann found a hideout at the Querleitnerhof, a farmstead halfway up a mountain in the Salzburg Alps, an hour and a half distant from the nearest village. It was still not far enough. Nearly every

Hitler posing with the Bormann and Speer children, and others. (Bayerische Staatsbibliothek Bildarchiv)

day a jeep would crawl up from the valley bristling with heavily armed military police who searched rooms, stables and barns in pursuit of hidden SS personnel.

For the time being they showed no interest in the boy who passed them, driving the cows up to pasture. In truth, they could hardly have imagined that this nondescript teenager – christened Martin Adolf on 19 April 1930 – had Adolf Hitler as a godfather.

Nor did the farmer, Nikolaus Hohenwarter, suspect that the reason Martin muttered grace so quietly in his first days was that he didn't know the words. It was only after a week or so that he had learned how to cross himself by

The father of the Reich and his children: Hitler was an unashamed exploiter of the dictator's great photographic cliché. (Bayerische Staatsbibliothek Bildarchiv)

watching the farmer, and only later that he was able to say out loud and clear: 'Our Father, who art . . .'

Gradually he forgot the words he had learned to say at table in Matrei: 'Let the weakling anxiously quail, he must dare who will prevail! Life is what we ask, or death – *Mahlzeit!*'

On Sundays he made the hour-and-a-half's journey down to Weissbach with Nikolaus Hohenwarter to go to Mass. In the beginning he did it merely to please the farmer. And because he couldn't easily say that he had no religion . . .

That summer of 1945, the farmer would occasionally

point across to a mountaintop on the far side of the valley. 'Over there you'll find the most beautiful church in our region – Maria Kirchtal.'

Only once did Nikolaus Hohenwarter have suspicions about Martin. It was one evening as the boy, just before going to sleep, suddenly said: 'What's going to happen to my mother?'

Your mother? thought Hohenwarter. (Martin, true to the Salzburg *Gauleiter*'s instructions, had used the cover story that his parents had lost their lives in a bombing raid.) But the farmer decided to ask no questions, and to wait till the boy decided to speak unprompted.

Bormann's mother was being held in the Untermais prison in Meran. She was interrogated almost without interruption by CIC officers.[1]

'Where is your husband?'

'Where is your eldest son?'

'Did they attempt to escape together?'

In Germany the Allies were preparing the ground for the Nuremberg trials. Apart from Hitler, Goebbels and Himmler who had all committed suicide, the Nazi leadership in its entirety was under lock and key. Only *Reichsleiter* Bormann was missing, and the Allies were determined to see him on the defendants' benches.

'I don't know anything,' said Gerda Bormann.

---

[1] Officers of the Combined Intelligence Committee, the joint US–British intelligence body.

She was not believed. Just as Hitler's chauffeur Kempka and the Reich youth leader Axmann had not been believed when they said that Bormann had fallen in the battle for Berlin. Intelligence officers will believe all kinds of explanations; the one thing they refused to believe was that a chance shellburst had done for the most cunning man in Hitler's entourage.

Her interrogators were unrelenting with Gerda Bormann.

'When did you last hear from your husband?'

'At the beginning of April, from Berlin –'

'Where is his hideout?'

'I don't know,' Gerda Bormann answered until she was exhausted. 'When can I go home to my children?'

'Not for the time being.'

'Can I at least write to them?'

'No.'

Their refusal plunged Gerda Bormann into despair. She had had to leave in a rush when the CIC had come for her in Gröden, leaving eight children behind. Joseph Volker was only a year old. Eicke was thirteen. Between them – like organ pipes – came Irma, Heinrich, Gerhard, Eva-Maria, Gerda and Friedrich Hartmut. Of Martin, the eldest, she had had no news.

In the end Frau Bormann was able to press a note into the hand of the prison chaplain, Theo Schmitz, who smuggled it out. The note was addressed to one Paula Pallhuber, Peroa, near Bruneck. 'Please take care of my children,' she wrote.

Paula Pallhuber, who from 1939 to 1944 had worked

as housekeeper at the Bormanns' villa in Munich-Pullach, straightaway packed her bags and went to Gröden to do as she was asked. Pallhuber, who has married since and become Paula Golderer, says today: 'I didn't think about it for a second. Frau Bormann was always a very good person.'

The Gröden house was under constant surveillance. Intelligence agents waited for Martin Bormann, war criminal, to get in touch with his children. The occupying powers had pasted up 200,000 notices throughout Germany calling on Bormann to make himself known, without success.

> Should he not appear, his case will be tried from 20 November onwards in his absence in the Palace of Justice in Nuremberg. Should he be found guilty, the sentence upon him will be carried out, in accordance with the orders of the Control Commission for Germany, without any further hearing, as soon as he has been found . . .

In the autumn of 1945 Frau Bormann was admitted to the prison hospital in Meran. She was seriously ill. The diagnosis exceeded her worst fears: she had abdominal cancer. She continued to be refused visits, to be prohibited from writing letters. Theo Schmitz, the prison chaplain, promised her on her deathbed to take care of her children.

Gerda Bormann died on 23 April 1946. Her son Martin was to hear of her death only a year later when he happened to read an article in the *Salzburger Nachrichten*.

Theo Schmitz telegraphed Gröden with the news. Paula Pallhuber left the two smallest children in a neighbour's care and, with the other six in tow, set out by train for Meran. They arrived at the exact moment the funeral was taking place.

There were no wreaths, no speeches. Still less was there a grave of her own for the wife of the most powerful Nazi after Hitler. In Meran's military cemetery a recently covered grave was opened once more. Gerda Bormann's last resting place is shared with one Lance-Corporal Horst Brügger.

In April 1946 the young Martin was still living under his assumed name at the lonely Querleitnerhof on the far side of the Loferer Steinberge. He knew nothing of his mother's death. He had no idea where his brothers and sisters were. He read in the paper that his father had been tried as a war criminal in his absence.

Then he read the death sentence. The same evening he confessed his true identity to the farmer Nikolaus Hohenwarter.

Hohenwarter should have told the police. Instead he went to the priest at Weissbach. The priest at Weissbach discussed the matter with the priest at Maria Kirchtal.

Father Regens of Maria Kirchtal took the son of *Reichsleiter* Bormann under his care.

The young Bormann converted to Catholicism. For the second time in his life he was christened Martin. On this occasion it took place beneath the sign of the cross, whereas seventeen years before it had been a swastika . . .

In the surroundings of Maria Kirchtal and under the influence of Father Regens, Martin rapidly resolved to enter the priesthood. He became a ministrant and applied to the Disciples of the Heart of Jesus for admission to their seminary. By return of post he was informed of the conditions of entry: he must show a sincere intention to become a Heart of Jesus missionary, a good aptitude, sincere godliness, good character and health – specifically, he should also be free from mental disorders, tuberculosis and bedwetting, similarly any ailment that was disfiguring or otherwise repellent . . . The only other exclusions, the letter noted, were boys of illegitimate birth, pupils expelled from any educational institution, and boys whose parents might one day expect material support from them.

Nothing stood in the way of Martin's entry to the seminary. He was only delayed for a few weeks by the sudden realisation of US intelligence of who exactly was ministering at Mass in the pilgrims' church at Maria Kirchtal.

Bormann junior was arrested and transferred to a prison at Zell am See. The interrogations lasted several days. Always the same questions.

'Where is your father?'

'When did you last see him?'

'Was he in Salzburg at the end of the war?'

'Is he living in Austria? Italy? Where? Tell us!'

But Martin didn't tell. He knew nothing. Despite all the interrogation, no trace could be found to link the son to the father. The fate of Bormann senior remained as shrouded in mystery as before, and Martin junior had to be released. He returned to Maria Kirchtal until, with a suitcase that contained all his earthly goods, he moved to the Heart of Jesus Missionaries in Ingolstadt where, along with the other boys, he offered the prescribed prayer: 'Lord, let me become an enlightened priest, in accordance with the example of Thy most sacred heart! Lord, reward the parents who have given me to Thee . . .'

Before Martin left Austria, he was able to resume contact with his brothers and sisters. The prison and army chaplain Theo Schmitz, who had promised Frau Bormann on her deathbed to take care of her children, kept his word, arranging the following foster homes:

Martin Bormann in 1960, two years after his ordination as a priest. The photo on his desk is of his father. (Hulton Getty)

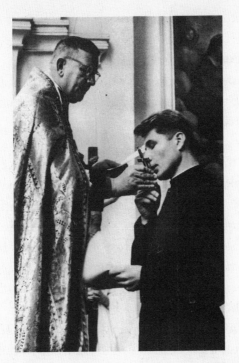

Bormann as a young missionary, receiving the blessing of the Father Provincial at Eichstätt in 1961, before leaving for the Congo. (Popperfoto)

Eicke was taken in by a Dr Kiener in Bruneck in South Tyrol.

Irma went to a timber merchant named Hellweger near St Lorenz.

Gerda and Eva-Maria found a new home with a Baroness Giovanelli in Bolzano.

Gerhard and Friedrich Hartmut were taken by Paula Pallhuber to her parents' in the village of Percha in the Pustertal.

Heinrich was found a place with farmers by the name of Mutschlechner in Saint Martin, also in the Pustertal.

The two-year-old Joseph Volker was looked after by the Bellenzier family, also farmers, in Luns near Bruneck.

Seven of the eight Bormann children were received into the Catholic Church that year, 1946. Only Irma refused.

Having found homes for the children, Father Theo Schmitz continued to follow the fortunes of *Reichsleiter* Bormann's children. Little Joseph Volker died before his third birthday. He suddenly stopped eating and lost weight. Frau Bellenzier, the farmer's wife, took him to Bruneck hospital. He lived another month in hospital, then the nurses placed him in a small coffin. Today you can read on a gravestone in the Dietenheim cemetery in the Pustertal, among the many Bellenziers, the words: 'Here lies the innocent foster child Joseph Volker Bormann.'

Although that inscription is already faded, there is another in a cemetery in Milan that is brand new and bears the name 'Eicke Moreni'. The Italians who walk past have no inkling that here lies the eldest daughter of Martin Bormann.

When Eicke Bormann arrived at her foster parents' in Bruneck at the age of fourteen, she was a difficult child. She was not only very like her father in appearance, she had also inherited parts of his nature: his ambition, his arrogance, his lust for power.

'We had our problems with her,' Frau Dr Kiener admits. 'She remembered her father very well and still thought he was a great man. She didn't want to hear about his guilt at all. She was used to luxury and thought she was still entitled to it. Eicke very much had the feeling of being something better. She used to tell stories to her brothers and sisters and classmates about the wonderful past. She was somehow proud to be a Bormann.'

Dr Kiener sent Eicke Bormann at his own expense to the English academy in Meran. There she worked not only hard, but doggedly. Every year she was top of her class. At seventeen when she began to put on puppy fat, she set herself a radical slimming programme and lost twenty pounds in a month.

After a glittering *Abitur* she attended teacher-training college. In 1953 she began teaching at the German school in Meran. Less than a year later, on 26 July 1954, she married Natalino Moreni, a chemist, in Milan.

'Her marriage changed Eicke very much for the better,' as Frau Kiener puts it. 'She lost her arrogance and ambition. She was happy, and she showed us she was grateful to us too. She and her husband spent their honeymoon with us in Bruneck.'

The Morenis lived in a three-roomed apartment in the via Silico Italico in Milan. On 24 September 1955 they announced the birth of their daughter Elisabeth. Their happiness lasted another two years, then Eicke Moreni was admitted to hospital with Werlhof's disease. She died on 4 July 1958.

Dr Natalino Moreni married again in April 1959.

Today he has two children with his second wife. Eicke's daughter Elisabeth lives in a children's home on Lake Garda. Following in her mother's footsteps, she too is likely to be looking for foster parents soon . . .

'I want to stay the way my father was' – the phrase is Irma's, the second oldest Bormann daughter. As a young impressionable girl, she got her head well stocked with National Socialist attitudes. All attempts to win her over to the Catholic faith failed. She was lucky with her foster father Hellweger, whom she called 'Uncle'. He paid for her private secondary school and her teacher-training college. But like her sister, Irma did not teach for long. In 1957 she married a cabinet-maker named Klotz and lives today at number 47 Romerstrasse in Meran. Since her marriage she has fallen out with her foster parents. 'We've had enough of her,' says Frau Hellweger. 'We don't want to see her face here again.'

Hartmut, who went with Paula Pallhuber to the Pustertal, had no memories of the family home. He called his foster parents 'Father' and 'Mother' and felt happy and comfortable at the farm. 'Hartmut was a nice hard-working lad,' Alois Pallhuber, a farmer and timber merchant, says today about his foster son. Hartmut now works as an apprentice salesman in Essen.

All the Bormann children, apart from Joseph Volker, grew to adulthood. Eva-Maria is a saleswoman in Berger's furniture store in Bolzano, Heinrich drives heavy equipment in Duisburg, Gerda has a job as a lady's companion in Essen. They grew up as orphans, looked after by farmers, timber merchants, a baroness and a doctor in South

Tyrol. Of their father they know nothing. Most of them know him only from photographs in newspapers. They have no family album and no memory. They only bear his name.

They have had no confirmation that he is dead, nor any clue that he is still alive. He would be sixty this year. He would have four grown-up sons, three grown-up daughters and a sprinkling of grandchildren. But he would also have, were he to surface once more from the void, the death penalty ahead of him as expiation for his crimes. 'Should he be found guilty, the sentence upon him will be carried out, in accordance with the orders of the Control Commission for Germany, without any further hearing . . .'

Martin Bormann junior was ordained on 26 July 1958 with twenty-five other deacons in the University Church in Innsbruck, as a priest of the Society of Missionaries of the Most Sacred Heart of Jesus. In the Second World War fifty-eight missionaries from the Order died in Japanese concentration camps. In southern China, seven were murdered by communists.

The young priest applied to be posted to Coquilhatville in the Belgian Congo, an appallingly poor territory, with only fifteen missionaries to care for 150,000 inhabitants.

On the left, by the sofa, hangs a silver-framed photograph of Heinrich Himmler. You see it as soon as you enter the small apartment. In any other apartment in the Federal Republic, you would be amazed beyond measure. In this place, however, it was to be expected.

For on Father Martin Bormann's writing desk there also stood a portrait of *Reichsleiter* Martin Bormann. 'I am his son,' the priest replies to difficult questions from reporters.

And Gudrun Himmler, whose apartment in Munich this is, is the daughter of *Reichsführer-SS* Heinrich Himmler.

The eldest Bormann son and Himmler's only daughter are almost identical in age. They played together as children. When their fathers' regime collapsed, they were both fifteen. They had been brought up in the same spirit. They sang the same songs. Today they have only one thing left in common: their fathers' portraits in their rooms. The young Bormann, still fighting in early May 1945 in the Loferer mountains with a gun in his hand, has changed over the years. He has put a great distance between himself and his past. He has become a Christian, a priest and a missionary. He prays today for his father.

Gudrun Himmler, however, is determined to fight for her father. 'I look on it as my life's work to show him to the world in a different light. Today my father is branded as the greatest mass murderer of all time. I want to try to revise this image. At least to get the facts straight about what he thought and why he acted as he did.'

A Priest Offers a Warning
about the Future

I GO TO see Martin Bormann. He seems to be a decent man: a very friendly person anyhow. Before our meeting was finally arranged, we exchanged several letters. In his last fax he had related how he had been in Israel again a few days previously and been present at a meeting of an encounter group of children of Holocaust survivors and children of perpetrators of Nazi crimes, a group led by the Israeli psychologist Dan Bar-On. On this occasion there had also been guests from other countries: South Africa, Northern Ireland, the Palestinian territories. One day they had been taken to a refugee camp in Bethlehem. Roughly 100,000 people, 85 per cent of them unemployed, lived in the camps, Bormann wrote. 'And what will happen to these people in the years to come?'

For weeks and months, books on the subject of National Socialism have been piling up in my apartment. On my bedside table there's a copy of *My Father: A Reckoning* by Niklas Frank, black-bound with red Gothic script, and of *Crying After an Execution – Getting Closer to My Father Panzermeyer, Major-General of the Waffen-SS*, in which a fifty-year-old son recognises over and over again how deeply his life has been stamped by his father. In the living room there's a copy of *The Nuremberg Trials* by Joe Heydecker and Johannes Leeb and of *The Price of Glory* by Henriette von Schirach. I don't seem to be able to remove from the toilet my copy of *In the Gallows' Gaze*, containing the many last words of Hans Frank, and in the kitchen there's the Hess biography by Wolf-Rüdiger, with the excellent title *I Have No Regrets*. In my local bookshop in Berlin they know me well. With every Nazi book I buy there, my worries increase as to what the nice, pleasant woman at the cash desk must be thinking: why is he buying all this stuff? One day, as I found myself ordering the euphoric biography of Göring by David Irving – the much disputed British Nazi researcher – I said something like: 'I need it for professional reasons: obviously it's not for my own pleasure . . .' 'Of course, obviously,' she replied with a cool smile.

It's a strange feeling for me to be reading and writing about National Socialism all day, every day. I make mental notes about what music I listen to with which book. With *Mein Kampf* it was jazz – Dexter Gordon. It was mostly jazz. It was Herbie Hancock when I was reading Gitta Sereny's biography of Albert Speer and came across the views of a gentleman named Theodor Hupfauer. Hupfauer had been a close colleague of Speer's; he was very old, over ninety, when Mrs Sereny interviewed him in the early 1990s. So that she should know straight away, Hupfauer said, he didn't take back one centimetre of his convictions from that time; not one. He remained a Nazi, and furthermore had recently been in the best of spirits, having noticed that so much nowadays was coming back from those days. Did he mean the skinhead movement? What was she talking about? asked Hupfauer. No, he meant today's youth culture, fine young people who wanted to be man and woman again, husband and wife, that pleased him. The all-decisive power of youth: 'We couldn't have put it better ourselves.' And he wanted someone to explain to him the difference 'between our euthanasia policy' and the current practice of allowing the termination of pregnancy on the basis of testing positive for certain handicaps. 'I don't see any great difference between the two.'

Maybe jazz is the music that best helps me keep my distance from such talk: a distance I occasionally need and long for. Because the more time and energy I spend on the subject, fifty-five years after the downfall of the Third Reich, the clearer it becomes to me that it isn't even a question of whether we might have spent too long remembering something so that now, or some time soon, we will have to call a halt. It's about something else, the fact that in a certain way, National Socialism answered certain questions. The answers were: anti-Semitism, xenophobia, cults of youth and body, the meaning of life, exaltation of the small man, anti-intellectualism, anti-politics. Answers formulated by Nazism and the Nazis in the most extreme way. Such a thing shall never happen again. But the answers are as current as they ever were. If it's true that communism will never lose its currency, so long as the gulf remains between rich and poor, fascism is subject to exactly the same law.

I was at the cinema recently to see *Fight Club*, a Hollywood production starring Edward Norton and Brad Pitt. A successful movie and certainly a good one from cinematographic and technical points of view. As I say, maybe I've been reading too much, but with negligibly transposed details of time and place, the movie's story could have come straight from the early years of the Nazi enterprise. A young man despairs of his hollow, meaningless life and the meaningless society around him. With another bloke who is apparently his friend, he founds the so-called Fight Club, where young, mostly very good-looking guys get together to beat the daylights out of each other. They hit each other in order to feel something, to feel alive again. All over the country other secret clubs are formed – fighting units, like the SS or SA. Finally they all attack together, striking against the state, terrorists of the new meaning of life. When I leave the cinema, I want to ask Klaus von Schirach, the son of the Hitler Youth leader, what he thinks of the movie, whether it reminds him of anything about the past and about his father. But that comes later.

The train for Dortmund leaves at eight a.m., an express named *Graf Stauffenberg*. On the journey I reflect how (relatively) well things were going for my father's generation when he was writing his pieces. When he met the young Martin Bormann, for example. The tail end of the 1950s: the middle of the great repression. Everything pointed to the future, as people then thought of it, no one looked back into the past. People were creating distance. Not long ago the distinguished Bochum historian Norbert Frei published an extensive investigation on the subject of coming to terms with the past, and the result startled even an experienced modern historian like him. The extent to which Germans, at every social level, on the one hand no longer wanted to think about the past and on the other believed that most of the evildoers should be reassimilated, harmoniously and without fuss, was breathtaking.

My father also kept his distance in his stories. He refused to allow the dark years to get too close. He described the Nazi children with emotion, yet coolly, as figures between two epochs, somehow helplessly marooned on the summit of Germany's bloody history.

Martin Bormann is waiting for me at Dortmund station, as arranged. Thick white hair and a brown, tanned face. The nearly seventy-year-old man looks dazzlingly well; in brown corduroy trousers and a checked shirt he looks like a model South Tyrolean mountain farmer. He says he occasionally has problems with his skin, a nerve-related dermatitis that is helped by regular exposure to Alpine sun. We walk to his car: the small town where he has lived for many years is about forty kilometres distant.

There's a piece of gold paper stuck inside the car, a document issued by the Association for Safe Driving. It is a handsome certificate, so handsome that I harbour a suspicion that there must be some story, possibly painful, behind it.

And so it turns out: Bormann has been involved in a serious car accident, one that, given the severity of his injuries, he was extremely lucky to survive. It happened on 25 April 1971. He had already lived a substantial life. He had spent years in Africa as a missionary in the middle of a bloody civil war in the Congo. He had returned home at the end of the 1960s on the grounds of ill health, and was working in Germany as a kind of roving lecturer and speaker about things spiritual and divine. He was driving his brand-new Opel Rekord near a place called Vilseck in the Bavarian Oberpfalz. Atrociously stormy weather had just set in, and when for a second or two at a junction motorists were blinded by sheeting rain, a near head-on smash occurred between an American army truck and the white Opel. Bormann awoke ten days after the collision in intensive care.

As his condition began to improve, he was told that he owed his life to a mechanic who had witnessed the accident by chance from his nearby workshop and managed to prise open the wreck of the Opel with a crowbar, far enough for him to be pulled clear. Oh, and there was another piece to the story, that the mechanic had told the clinic he had once known Martin Bormann junior, long before, when he was an eleven-year-old boy.

It was true: his rescuer had for several years been chauffeur to *Reichsführer-SS* Heinrich Himmler, and in that incarnation had more than once driven Martin and two of his sisters to Himmler's house on the Tegernsee. (The reason for the visits was coffee mornings organised by the mothers.) That Himmler's former driver should have saved his life leads Bormann in his autobiography to write of 'intervention in the skeins of destiny' and of 'a gift of God's providence'. Of course people always tend to describe such escapes as 'fateful'. But one could just as easily say that the past had once more signalled its presence, albeit in an unexpected way.

Himmler's name and home have a particular – a particularly grisly – significance for Martin Bormann. About a year before the end of the war he and his sisters were at the house at the Tegernsee, on a visit with their mother. Suddenly Himmler's secretary (and lover) Hedwig Potthast said, with solemn excitement, that she wanted to show them all something very interesting: a very personal collection of her boss's. Taking them upstairs to the attic floor, she opened a room. In it stood tables and chairs made from human body parts. One of the chair seats was made of a carved and polished pelvic girdle, another had legs made from human legs, complete with human feet. Then Frau Potthast showed them a copy of *Mein Kampf* bound with skin from a human back. Bormann remembers, as if it were yesterday, how clinically and medically it was all explained. And how shocked and petrified he and his sisters he had been and how, once they were outside, their equally stricken mother tried to comfort them by telling them that Himmler had wanted to send their father one of his specially bound copies of *Mein Kampf* and that, horrified, he had refused it. It had been too much for him, really, their mother said. One feels like adding: even for him.

We're sitting in a quiet restaurant somewhere in

Westphalia, a place Bormann likes to come to whenever he is being interviewed. 'They know me here. "Ah," they say, "here comes Herr Bormann again."' He has really only interested himself in his father's life and work since his retirement; before, he shied away from publicity. 'I didn't like people discussing my name.' Today, he says, he reads everything he can get his hands on about the Third Reich. He is the only one in his family who wants to know the full story of Martin Bormann senior. Six brothers and sisters are still alive (the twins have died, as has one of the sisters). 'When we're together,' says Martin, 'we never talk about old times. They know my book, they know what I'm doing. If they were to ask me, I'd tell them, but they don't ask. Maybe it's still too early. Maybe some day the grandchildren will come.'

Martin junior had an awkward birth, so to speak: he was born to fall. And the extraordinary thing about him is that he grabbed perhaps the only chance not to fall: he became a Christian, he clutched God's hand. He himself naturally sees things differently: it was God who clutched his hand. When he was at rock bottom, he was saved. Like Jesus making the lame man walk. So he says.

Despite such explanations, his life was not simple. You can see it in his hands, often balled tightly during our conversation, a bit too tightly as though they had to hold something together that is constantly threatening to fall apart.

The damn past. His godfather was Adolf Hitler. Of course he remembers him. Martin was the eldest, lovingly nicknamed Kronzi, short for Crown Prince. On the

Obersalzberg he often played go-between, carrying letters between the Führer and his father. Martin junior says
that whenever Hitler walked into a room, it suddenly felt
cold, as though everything in the room was freezing. Once
he muffed the Hitler salute, saying something like 'Heil
Führer', and nearly had his head knocked off by his
father.

'You know,' Martin says more than once during our
conversation, 'you never escape from your parents, whoever they are.' In 1948 or 1949 he read a report in the
newspaper. Bormann – Hitler's secretary – it said, was
alive and living in Moscow; the truth could now be told
that he had always been Stalin's mole in the Führer's headquarters. It was, of course, complete rubbish, but the first
thing Martin junior thought as he read was: If it's true,
then my father, the great church-hater, knows I have
become a Christian and where I live. If it's true, then we're
now enemies. There is no other word for it: Martin was
afraid.

In Africa, some time in 1964, working as a missionary,
he was taken hostage and found himself in a dangerous
situation, from which he was rescued by Belgian para-
chutists at the eleventh hour. When he reached the airport
at Leopoldville, reporters were waiting for him. But the
utterly exhausted and relieved Martin Bormann was
asked nothing about his experiences or his rescue. What
the reporters wanted to know was what he had to say
about the Frankfurt public prosecutor's publication of a
bounty of 100,000 Deutschmarks for information leading
to his father's whereabouts. He said nothing.

Martin Bormann quit his religious order at the beginning of the 1970s. He married and worked as a divinity teacher. In the ordinary run of things, he should have taken up a post at a vocational college at Mühldorf in Bavaria, a post he had been recommended for by the college faculty; but the admissions committee turned him down flat. Behind the scenes, the reason was not difficult to discern – in Bavaria particularly, the name Bormann still had a nasty ring to it. Not so much because of the crimes of National Socialism – though of course there was all that too – but mainly because so many Berchtesgaden farms had been ruthlessly expropriated by Bormann senior. At this point the *Spiegel* magazine began to talk of trial by kinship, and in 1973 Martin junior got his new post – in Westphalia.

Martin Bormann has erected a kind of scaffolding for his life. On the one side there is his father to whom he owes his existence, a father he still loves, even today. Fourth commandment: Thou shalt honour thy father and mother. On the other is a father named Martin Bormann who committed terrible crimes and bore a heavy burden of guilt. This man he regards with a severe and critical eye – to put it mildly and carefully. Of course the scaffolding is held up by religion: who or what else could sustain it? Bormann says that it is not for men to judge other men. That is God's business alone.

Is not this structure somewhat schizophrenic? It may well sound like it, Bormann agrees, 'but for me it isn't, for me it is the one and only possibility'. In saying so, he is not embarking on any kind of attempt to diminish his father's guilt. He has no illusions. His father was sentenced to death *in absentia* at Nuremberg. Was there any chance, did he think, that had he defended himself as Hess and Speer had done, he might have got off with a long jail sentence? 'No,' is Martin's answer. 'His signature was on too many important documents and orders. No, today you've got to say it loud and clear. My father knew everything that was going on.'

How does he feel then, when he sees his father depicted in practically every document of the Nazi era, every report or book, as the embodiment of pure evil, impersonal, brutal, scheming, ready for God knows what infamy? I ask the question, and his reaction surprises me. He has certainly been too controlled, too self-possessed, perhaps too on top of the situation during our talk. Now he is upset, and he seems in danger of losing his temper and his poise. His hands wring and clench. He pulls his wallet from his trouser pocket, finds an old yellowed postcard and takes it out. A few words are scribbled on it, written by his father in 1943. 'Look,' he says. There are tears in his eyes. 'My darling boy,' it says. 'I hope I'll be able to see you again soon. Your Daddy.'

'Can you understand,' says Bormann, 'that's the picture I have of him as his son? I won't let anyone take that away from me. I set that against everything.'

The man sitting in front of me is elderly, a couple of months short of his seventieth birthday. One cannot reproach him with making things easy for himself. He has organised his life so that the older he gets, the more arduous it has become. Although he is a pensioner, he voluntarily drives all over Germany, giving lectures in schools and elsewhere about the dangers of National Socialism. There are many cities in eastern Germany where he needs police protection. He says he doesn't believe that its appalling ideology is over and done with: 'We must take great care.'

Bormann relates how in his victims' and perpetrators' groups he has seen the perpetrators' children, often people over fifty, break down completely and utterly when they stop repressing their inheritance and are able to face up to it. One scene in particular has remained in his memory. A woman was showing a video. It documented the day of her father's release from prison, a man sentenced a few years after the war's end to a prison term of several years for hideous crimes he had committed as a doctor. His first day on the outside: the viewer saw him coming home, the viewer saw him walk with a fairly sprightly step in through the front door of his house and greet his family: 'Heil Hitler!'

The Israeli psychologist Dan Bar-On, whose family fled from Berlin to Palestine in 1933, travelled to Germany at the end of the 1980s to break the taboo of why it was that, in a country of such evildoers, there was no talk of how the acts they had committed were dealt with by their children? Before formally assembling his discussion groups, Bar-On had conducted a number of long interviews with some of the descendants, conversations which were recorded in part in his book *The Burden of Silence*.

In conversation with Martin Bormann he puts a question to the theologian and churchman:

Bar-On: 'Has anyone ever confessed to you or to one of your fellow priests any atrocities they took part in during the extermination process?'

Bormann: 'No, I can't think of anyone . . . though yes, there was one situation, though I'm not sure it's exactly what you're looking for. A man came to me shortly before he died. In his confession he told me that in all the years since it had happened, the brown eyes of a six-year-old girl had given him no peace. He had been in the *Wehrmacht*, he was serving in Warsaw at the time of the uprising in the ghetto. They had been ordered to clear out the bunkers, and one morning a six-year-old girl came running towards him out of one of these bunkers, her arms outstretched. He still remembered the look in her eyes, terrified and full of trust at the same time. Then his NCO ordered him to bayonet her, which he did. He killed her. But the look in her eyes haunted him for the rest of his life [Bormann's voice begins to break and his eyes fill with tears]. And he came to me to confess it – he had never told anyone about it before.'

(A long pause.)

Bar-On (weeping): 'Tell me: perhaps you can help me to understand. Why was it just those eyes? Why didn't he remember the eyes of all the others whom he had perhaps also killed? And why was he the only one to confess? What did all the others do about the eyes of the women and children that looked at them helplessly before they were killed? And can you tell me how this man could keep that memory to himself all that time?'

Bormann: 'I don't know, I have no answers, I can only suppose they all had some kind of feeling of guilt that came to them at different times. But I really don't have any answers to your questions . . .'

Dan Bar-On, with whom Martin Bormann later became friends, writes at the end of this conversation: 'As we walked to the bus stop together, we were both deep in our own feelings and thoughts again . . . I watched him as he walked away. A great burden seemed to be balanced on his shoulders, a great weight lay on his heart. I felt his profound involvement and his feeling of responsibility for what had happened during his father's time.'

Our time together is drawing to an end. We have sat talking for several hours. He drives me back to Dortmund station. I glance at him. The slightly hunched shoulders, the controlled, sometimes practically stony expression on his face: what Dan Bar-On wrote still holds true, the weight is there still. He will probably take it with him to the grave.

Nazi children. Bormann says he had things easier than, for example, Wolf-Rüdiger Hess. 'My father was gone for ever. It was easier for me to set a boundary.' He tells the story of how Gudrun Himmler, Himmler's daughter, once phoned him in a rage. She screamed at him: How could he make such terrible remarks about the old times? Bormann says that he tried to explain to her that their fathers and their fathers' deeds were two different things. She didn't understand. 'I don't think she has quite got that far yet.'

It is the former priest talking now. Martin Bormann junior says he would like to get to know Niklas Frank one day: Frank, the son who decided to take the path of hate. How does he see it? Can things work that way? 'So much hatred,' he says, then, 'I'd like the chance to talk to him. Maybe I could help him.'

The 1959 Manuscript:

NIKLAS AND NORMAN FRANK

'I'M GLAD MY father was spared Spandau. If he'd been imprisoned like that he would probably have been utterly broken, a wreck by now. As it is, we got over his death a long time ago and my father's ashes have been cast to the four winds – so I come across him everywhere.'

The young man who speaks these words is called Niklas Frank. He is twenty-one years old and a student, as his father once was, at the Munich law faculty. His father was Hans Frank, one-time governor-general of Poland, principal defendant number seven at the International Military Tribunal at Nuremberg. When he was hanged on 16 October 1946, he left five children. Niklas was the youngest. He had just started in his second year at the *Volksschule*.

'I hold my father guilty. He committed dreadful crimes and paid for them with his death. He himself realised that in his final days and left us children his admission of guilt as his legacy, so to speak.' The words of Norman Frank, the eldest son of the former governor-general of Poland. Today the thirty-two-year-old works as an assistant director in the movie business. In 1945, when his father was arrested, he was no longer a boy.

I sit facing the two brothers in an apartment in Schwabing. They don't look alike, nor do they bear any resemblance to their father. Niklas sports a ginger student's beard that makes him look a couple of years older. Their mother died eighteen months ago. Nothing has been changed in the apartment since her death. The old furniture, the pictures and carpets are all from their parents, and outside, on the brass plate on the door, there's still the father's name, Hans Frank. The brass plate has accompanied them on all their moves in recent years.

Niklas Frank, for whom the theatre is his one true love, vacillated at length before embarking on his law studies. 'My father's fate somehow tipped the scales. But don't misunderstand me. I'm not studying law so that I can rehabilitate him.' Niklas considers a moment. 'I'd like to get my own picture of him. I'll study the trial records from Nuremberg, read his diaries, look for the Polish documents . . . I want to get to know him.'

The Frank sons are not burying their heads in the sand. They aren't shying away from a showdown with the past. On the contrary, that is exactly what they are looking for.

'Unfortunately my father loved power above everything,' says Norman Frank. 'Just imagine – at my age he was already Bavarian justice minister. Two years later he was *Reichsminister*. Then they crowned him king of Poland . . .'

It was not until the Nazis' power collapsed that Hans Frank realised how disastrous his path had been.

'This is merely the humble confession of guilt for the murder of several million innocent people,' he wrote in pencil in an exercise book in his prison cell. He disputed none of the facts about his crimes. He converted to the Catholic faith, and in the company of an Irish Franciscan priest named Sixtus O'Connor walked, praying aloud, his final steps to the gallows.

'My dear Norman,' began the letter addressed to the eldest Frank son by Father O'Connor the night after the executions.

Allow me to extend my hand in spirit to you and to your courageous mother and brothers and sisters, in silent sympathy for the passing of your dear father. On the eve of his death I was with him. We made our devotions together, and I read him the Sermon of Christ on the Mount of Olives. Afterwards we talked for a short time, and then your father went to bed. Just before midnight he was woken up and informed that his execution would take place shortly. Just after 24.00 hours I gave him holy communion. During his last fifteen minutes I spoke with him, then gave him the last rites and complete absolution. He was quite calm and resigned, and charged me to send his greetings to your mother, you and your brothers and sisters and to say that he had taken death willingly unto himself as a penance and in atonement for the past. His last thoughts were of all of you. However, he had no anxiety about you. He was convinced that you understand everything and that you will also, with courage and your faith in God, stay on top of life in the future.

Before we left the cell, I made a small sign of the cross on his forehead, his mouth and his chest – as his mother always used to bless him when he was a boy on his way to school. On the way to the place of execution we prayed to St Joseph for a good death. Once there, he made the following statement: 'I am grateful for the kind treatment shown to me during my imprisonment, and I ask the Lord God to be pleased to receive me in His mercy.' I read him a short prayer, and at the end he said: 'My Jesus, have mercy.' Those were his last words. Two hours after his death I offered funeral prayers and read a Mass.

I feel certain that your father went straight to Heaven and that before the throne of God's judgment he found a fair hearing. Now he has most decidedly found the rest and peace and love that this world cannot give. To you, however, dear Norman, there remains the duty of carrying on your father's name in this world and of continuing to defend his honour . . .

The Irish priest's letter is kept today, somewhat yellowed, in the family album. Fourteen years have gone by since then. There has never been any other news from Father O'Connor. Niklas Frank would like to track him down.

'Even if I have to go to America,' he says. 'Father O'Connor is definitely the person who knows most about my father.'

Before the war the Franks lived in Munich. In 1938 Norman started at the Max Gymnasium where, twenty years earlier, his father had passed his *Abitur* with distinction. In 1940 the family moved to Warsaw. Until 1943 Norman went to the German school there, until he was evacuated to Czechoslovakia in 1944. That year Brigitte Frank travelled with her five children back to Germany. They lived at the Schoberhof, a large detached house on the Schliersee that Frank had bought years before. Norman attended secondary school at Miesbach.

There was a problem: most of the time the sixteen-year-old Norman failed to turn up at Hitler Youth meetings. His mother had a difficult time explaining his absences to the local group leader. She had further difficulties when Norman was found for the third time with banned jazz records. 'I didn't care for parades or any of that kind of thing,' says Norman. 'We were much happier listening to records in cellars.'

On 22 January 1945 Hans Frank, Poland's governor-general, tactically withdrew to the Schliersee and set up a reduced headquarters for himself in Neu-Josephstal. He was arrested there on 1 May by an American army patrol.

Thin, watery snow lay on the roads as Norman pedalled from the Schoberhof to Josephstal. The American armoured spearhead was expected at any moment. For months the boy had been listening in secret to the enemies' broadcasts: '. . . all the war criminals will be brought to account'. He suspected his father of belonging to this group.

Numb with cold, he entered his father's headquarters. The Führer's portrait still hung on the wall. Secretaries were talking on the phones. Staff officers came and went. Everything was as normal . . .

'Good timing, Norman,' said Hans Frank, 'you can join us for coffee. Another cup, please.'

The table was laid. There were even cakes from somewhere. Coffee and cakes in the King of Poland's private quarters on the afternoon of 1 May . . .

The conversation was friendly and relaxed between Frank, a few colleagues, secretaries and Norman. The governor-general was in a joking mood.

'I must be the only minister who is looking forward to his own arrest quite so cheerfully.'

'Are you sure it'll come to that, *Herr Minister*?' someone asked.

'I believe so. But when it happens I shall hand over my diaries. Every day is accounted for. I'm extremely glad I possess that record. I have nothing to fear.'

Frank was calm, almost lighthearted. He showed not the faintest trace of nerves. Gone was the nervousness he had shown so openly a few years before. It was at a celebratory dinner in Cracow: between the salmon and stuffed pigeon he had suddenly announced to his guests with forced cheerfulness: 'My astrologer told me today

127

that my stars look very bad, that I'm going to die a violent and dreadful death –'

'Americans, two kilometres from the Schliersee,' a girl now began shouting through all the doors.

The coffee party broke up. The governor-general's remaining colleagues melted quietly away. Only Norman stayed with his father. Through field glasses they scanned the lakeside road from the window.

'There they are!' said Norman excitedly. The first tank, three, four or more Jeeps behind it bristling with machine pistols. Soldiers, round steel helmets, khaki uniforms.

'You go home now,' Hans Frank ordered. 'I expect I'll be back home with you all soon.'

The war diaries that Frank handed over that afternoon to an American officer amounted, as far as the prosecutors of Nuremberg were concerned, to a dossier of such incriminating evidence that it needed no further elaboration. They contained for example the following entries:

19 January 1940

I have received the order to ransack the conquered eastern territories ruthlessly, to transform their economic, social, cultural and political structure into a pile of smoking ruins.

9 September 1941

. . . research shows that the greater part of the Polish population consumes only around 600 calories a day, while the usual requirement for a human being is 2200 calories. The Polish population is so severely debilitated that it is becoming an easy prey to fatal infection . . . Our general principle is that we sympathise only with our own German people and with no one else in the world.

15 October 1941

. . . no further food supplies will be made available to the Jewish population.

24 August 1942

. . . that we are condemning 1.2 million Jews to death by starvation is only to be noted in passing.

2 June 1943

We began here with three and a half million Jews; of those we now have only a few labour companies left, all the rest have – let us say – emigrated.

25 January 1943

I want to emphasise one thing: we should not be squeamish when we hear the figure of 17,000 shot and killed . . . It would be foolish to allow arguments about our methods to start circulating at this stage.

12 January 1944

Once we have won the war, as far as I'm concerned the Poles and the Ukrainians and whoever else is knocking about can be turned into mincemeat.

'I still find it incomprehensible', says Norman Frank today, 'that my father could assume for even a moment that his war diaries would exonerate him. He was a lawyer, after all . . .'

At the time, however, the seventeen-year-old still believed his father. 'I'll be home with you all soon,' he had said. That day the Frank children waited with their mother. At first of course they heard nothing from him, not for five months. Only a single rumour: that he had tried to commit suicide in his cell.

The Schoberhof was no safe refuge for the Frank family. One night, foreign workers freed from their labour camps by the Americans attacked the house, arriving in two large trucks and storming into the bedrooms. With their hands up Brigitte Frank and the children fled into the courtyard. Norman exchanged a silent glance with his mother and his eldest sister. They could expect the worst, he knew, because the men standing in front of them, machine pistols raised, were Poles.

'Against the wall!' shouted a hoarse voice.

There was no resisting the order. Brigitte Frank and her five children stood with their faces to the wall. The dog tore at its chain, barking furiously. Otherwise the night was silent. The men who had taken over the Schoberhof talked to one another quietly in Polish.

What were they discussing? Norman, having picked up snatches of the language in Warsaw, strained vainly to catch what was being said. The situation was worse than hazardous. The heavily armed Poles standing behind them had been deported to slave-labour camps in Germany by

Hans Frank, with his wife and son Niklas. (Ullstein
Bilderdienst)

his father. The wives and parents they had left behind at
home might easily be dead, murdered by Germans. Who
would make a fuss if these men were to bump off the
family of the hated governor-general?

'Where's Frank?' A stocky young man who showed a
gold tooth when he spoke stood next to Norman.

'We don't know,' he replied.

'You've hidden him here!'

'No, the Americans arrested him.'

'We'll find him!' threatened the youth with the gold
tooth, apparently the only one who spoke German.

The adult Niklas Frank. (Niklas Frank)

The Poles began to turn the house upside down. They rifled every cupboard and corner, from attic to cellar. The cellar was well stocked, and at this discovery the Poles decided to taste the odd drop from the governor-general's collection of Mosel wine. They gradually gave less and less thought to the family up in the courtyard, instead slicing the necks off the bottles and getting thoroughly drunk. The Frank family, waiting with their faces to the wall, heard cheerful songs float up from the cellar. When the singing started, Gold-Tooth, who had been standing watch, shoved his machine pistol into his belt and slipped away to join his comrades.

'So we were able to make our getaway,' remembers Norman Frank. 'But we never felt safe at the Schoberhof again because an attack like that could have been repeated at any time.'

Brigitte Frank moved with her children to the next village, Neuhaus am Schliersee, where they managed to find a couple of rooms with a family named Hertlein. She was entitled to withdraw 300 Deutschmarks a month from her husband's blocked account. It was just enough to live on.

In August 1945 an American army newspaper published a report that the war criminal Hans Frank had made several attempts at suicide. Only three months earlier, he had said to his eldest son: 'I must be the only minister who is looking forward to his own arrest quite so cheerfully . . .'

In October the eldest Frank daughter, Sigrid, married and left home. And from Mondorf in Luxembourg there arrived a postcard written in block letters, informing them of Dr Hans Frank's presence in a camp at that location.

Almost simultaneously, his first letters began to arrive at Neuhaus. They show the one-time governor-general completely altered.

. . . ever gloomier is the night through which I must drag the dreadful burden of my cross. But God give me strength and faith . . .

. . . trusting in God without end, I live and know that you are all joined with me in prayer. The tests that life imposes on us admonish us for the manifold errors of our ways, but the Almighty looks into the depths and knows all truth. I hope you are all in good health, and I think of us all together in our old Schoberhof as the crowning moment of my hopes . . .

. . . mighty is fate, but mightier are those who bear it. Thus with God's help shall we accomplish all things. Day and night I think of you all in the unshakeable belief that we shall see each other once more . . .

'After these letters,' says Norman Frank, 'there was no doubt that our father had become a practising Catholic while in prison.'

'It must have come as a great surprise to you,' I say.

'Of course. Before, he had only been impressed by the power of the church. He often used to talk about it. Its worldwide organisation fascinated him. National Socialism ought to copy it, he said.'

'When did you yourself become a Catholic?'

'In 1944. After we came back from Warsaw, our mother had us all christened.'

Norman still remembered the Christmases spent with his father. 'When the bells rang for the service on Christmas morning, we all had to go out on the terrace. He acknowledged the bells with his right hand solemnly raised . . .'

In the autumn of 1945, as the prosecution of war-crimes defendant number seven Hans Frank was being prepared in Nuremberg, the secondary school at

Miesbach refused to accept his eldest son for the new term. Instead, a retired classical scholar named Dr Beermann tutored Norman for three hours a day, mainly in Greek. The results were not long in coming. When Norman presented himself for the *Abitur*, he passed in Greek but for maths handed in an empty paper. He failed.

His mother got him admitted to the Catholic boarding school at Metten. But within a short time he was home again. This time he had been punished for nothing more serious than setting up a jazz club. His younger brother Niklas was meanwhile in his last year at primary school. Michael was being looked after in a children's home.

One day in February 1946, Niklas failed to come home from school at the usual time.

Frau Frank looked for him around the village, then went to the schoolhouse. The classrooms were empty and the staff room was locked for the day. She eventually found the caretaker, who knew where Niklas was. 'He's in detention. I'm not supposed to let him out until one o'clock.'

'Why?' Brigitte Frank asked.

'He drew a swastika on the blackboard,' the caretaker replied.

Frau Frank asked for the detention room to be unlocked. 'Niklas, did you draw a swastika on the black-board?'

'No, Mum.'

'Why didn't you tell the teacher?'

'I told her. But she didn't believe me. I was the kind of boy who'd draw a swastika, she said.'

That story was soon forgotten. His brother Michael was the cause of a great deal more agitation. In March 1946 the director of the children's home sent a telegram to Neuhaus. It read: 'Michael missing since last night. Request answer has he arrived with you.'

The eight-year-old had not arrived. Nor did he arrive that evening.

Frau Frank ran to the police station. 'I don't hold out much hope,' said the policeman on duty with a shrug. He pointed to a stack of papers. 'Those are all the unsolved robberies. Where are we going to find the time to look for small children?'

'Can't you at least send out a telex?'

'Every telex has to be authorised by the occupying powers,' the police officer answered. 'The best thing would be an announcement on the radio. But to do that you need to know the right people.'

Brigitte Frank knew one person at the radio service, a man named Gaston Oulman. Every evening he broadcast a scathingly ironic commentary on the Nuremberg trials. Frau Frank had spoken to him only once. 'If you ever need help,' he had said to her unexpectedly, 'call me.'

She called Oulman at the Munich studios, and after the next news bulletin he broadcast a missing-persons announcement: 'An eight-year-old boy is missing. Blond, speaks with a Bavarian accent, wearing grey shorts and a red checked shirt . . .'

Michael Frank was picked up soon afterwards in Hamburg. He had wanted to board a ship for America, but had to be content with being put on a train by the police and sent back to Neuhaus.

The family was together again. From Nuremberg they continued to receive frequent letters. '. . . this morning at 10 o'clock we celebrated Mass in a small room in the building, simply but tastefully transformed into a chapel. Dear Father Sixtus officiated, and apart from myself there were only Seyss-Inquart and Herr von Papen – who ministered with the priest . . .'

Hans Frank had not yet given up hope. At the beginning of 1946 he was still writing: 'May this year finally see us all happily reunited . . .'

'At home we did not hold out very much hope any more,' says Norman Frank. 'Reports of the trial were looking worse than gloomy. On the Thursday before Easter my father admitted his guilt to the judges – what chance did he have after that?'

A fortnight before the verdicts were due, Brigitte Frank travelled to Nuremberg with her children. There were general visiting rights for the defendants' relations, and the families of the leading Nazis were lodged and fed by the Allies. They sat together, one last time, at long tables in a converted schoolroom.

It was their final appearance together. They were photographed and interviewed, as they had once been. In a macabre fashion they were centre-stage again.

Norman Frank remembers clearly the encounter with his father. 'Visiting time was restricted to a few minutes. The prisoners sat next to each other behind glass screens, flanked on either side by military police. He was handcuffed. My first impression was that there was a stranger in front of me. He had become very thin. His suit was flapping around him. His face had an almost ascetic quality.'

'Did he talk to you about the trial?'

'He said, "It's gone rather badly for me." But he gave the impression of considerable calm and composure.'

'So he was no longer holding out hope at this point?'

'No.'

'Death by hanging,' Lord Justice Lawrence, president of the tribunal, announced as expected to the accused Frank.

'During the night of 15 to 16 October I died,' were the last words of his last letter to his family.

A year later Norman Frank moved to Westphalia. He lived with relatives in a vicarage and worked as a wire-drawer in a factory. In the evenings he swotted up on physics and maths. He resat his *Abitur* at the Max Gymnasium in Munich, where his father had graduated as a model pupil. The twenty-one-year-old failed again and gave up.

In 1950 he left Germany and travelled. He sailed on the *Salta Liberty* to Buenos Aires and found a job as a ware-houseman in a tool factory. His boss was an émigré Pole.

'Are your views like your father's?' he asked Norman. 'Your father wanted to make mincemeat out of us.'

'No,' Norman replied Frank. 'I feel the opposite. I'm not a Nazi. I'm sorry that my father, of all people . . .'

'That's OK then,' said the Pole.

'I got on very well with him,' Norman asserts. 'Less well with the large number of Nazis in Argentina who wanted to pass me round like some sort of holy relic. Just because I'd once sat on Herr Hitler's lap.'

After nine months Norman travelled into the interior, to work first on a chicken farm, then in a lead mine on the Bolivian border. The lead pits lay in a lunar landscape, 5,000 metres above sea level. It took him some time to stop getting nosebleeds and headaches from the high altitude. Then he enjoyed the work so much that he stayed for three years. Incognito, since an Austrian doctor who had revealed that he was an ex-Nazi had immediately been fired without notice.

Shortly before the revolution that overthrew Peron, Norman Frank returned to Germany. Both his sisters had married. Michael was earning his livelihood as a car salesman. Niklas had just begun studying law.

Norman speaks today for all the Frank children when he says, 'We aren't going to undertake any action to recover any of my father's supposed assets. We must write all those kinds of things off, because they are loaded with guilt.'

A Man Wants to Destroy His Father

I'VE KNOWN NIKLAS Frank a long time. First as a reader, because for many years he's been working as a journalist at *Stern*. Niklas Frank is what he writes. In all his pieces there is a force you can feel, very often a sense of anger too. And then there was his *Stern* series 'My Father, the Nazi Murderer' which had a big impact and I can still remember an evening at home when my parents had a few people round and they were discussing this Niklas Frank person, as people did at that time in the Federal Republic – Niklas Frank was the current topic. The question being asked, at home and in plenty of other places, was: Is it permissible to treat your father the way Frank had treated his?

Frank's series in *Stern* had been a cry of rage. He had exceeded every boundary of journalistic restraint. He had written that every 16 October – the day of his father's hanging – he always masturbated over a photo of his dead daddy. He described unprecedented fantasies of hatred and murder he had conceived towards Herr Frank senior.

Here was a son dissecting his own father, going into the deepest recesses of his personality and delivering a devastating verdict: that his father was cowardly, corrupt, sexually stimulated by power, brutish, pampered, soft. There were no mitigating qualities. And with his words the son was also raging against himself. He had recognised his father's cowardice in himself, felt his father's heart beating in his own breast, and was tearing himself to shreds. Frank's articles, which were also published as a book, are a documentary exercise in tastelessness. Yet how could it have been otherwise, with Hans Frank as their subject, a man responsible for the deaths of several million people?

German public opinion at the time – this was in the mid-1980s – was broadly unanimous: the articles were sickening, the son a disgrace. Dozens of readers' letters appeared in *Stern*, all on the same theme: It doesn't matter what your father did, he's still your father and should be respected. Even left-wing commentators found Frank's outburst of emotion difficult to deal with; their usual response was: Well, it looks as though young Niklas has got a problem. Not a problem we need to discuss either; he should see a psychiatrist. It is interesting to note that one of the few positive reactions to what Frank wrote came from the American Robert M. W. Kempner, one of the prosecutors at Nuremberg. For months he had sat face to face with Hans Frank, had experienced this man from Hell in person. 'Niklas Frank's publication', Kempner wrote, 'is in its uniqueness an important contribution to the advancement of human rights.'

Klaus von Schirach, son of the Hitler Youth leader Baldur von Schirach, made a face when I mentioned Niklas Frank's name in his office in Munich. 'That devil!' Schirach said. 'That man has committed a sin that can never be atoned.' In Spain, he went on, there was a saying that whoever curses his parents is himself cursed for ever. 'I agree with this attitude.'

At our house that evening when Frank's name came up for discussion, the atmosphere was probably no different from anywhere else in Germany. From a family point of view, we had an interesting mix of guests present: one was the daughter of a high-ranking SS officer, another the daughter of a German Jew who had survived the Holocaust. Both were journalists, and were in accord: for Herr Frank to have wanked as a boy while thinking about his dead father, and then as a grown-up to tell the story, that was going too far. One shouldn't do such a thing, even in an extreme case like his.

I felt fairly indifferent to the discussion, as I generally did when the subject of National Socialism came up. I was fifteen or sixteen, and looking back I think I must have given the impression of being pretty dumb. Yeah, yeah, but it was all so long ago, of course it was terrible, but it's all over now – I was a teenager with no opinions, a boy who couldn't really understand why the grown-ups were getting so worked up.

But I still remember my father dissenting, and the fact that he was alone in his dissent. He felt sympathy for Frank, whom he had met as a young man, already embarked on his particular path of – what? Conquering the past? Reinventing it as a literary artefact? Traducing it? Tearing it up? My father also strongly approved of what Niklas Frank had written, and not just because it was well written. Maybe he knew all too well, after the research he'd carried out at the end of the 1950s, that anyone who wanted to overcome the Nazi past needed some sort of instrument of extreme force to do it.

One cold day in November 1999, I find myself telling Niklas Frank that my father had agreed with him. We're sitting in a small Italian restaurant not far from the Hamburg waterfront and the mighty *Stern* building, which, most likely because of its nearness to the water, reminds me of an ocean liner. I had waited in the lobby for Frank to descend from his office: sixty years old, married, one daughter, medium build, nearly bald, a reddish, close-clipped beard. Now he's eating a plate of *penne all'arrabiata* with a mixed salad, I'm eating *penne all'arrabiata* with a mixed salad. He replies: 'It's a shame your father didn't call and tell me. I could damn well have done with a bit of support, I can tell you. The reactions were as vehement as they come.' He remembers well that *Die Zeit* ran a piece under the headline of 'Frank the son, psychopath'. 'That hit me hard, it hurt me very much.' To protect himself, he withdrew, mentally and emotionally; in effect he froze inside. 'One day a colleague asked me in the lift at work, "How are things going these days, Niklas?" I had no idea what he was talking about, so tightly had I strapped on my armour.' It strikes me that Niklas Frank's precision as a reporter, observing others, probably comes from the knowledge he gained, experiencing everything a person is capable of doing to themselves.

When I wrote to him in the autumn of 1999 explaining in a couple of lines what I was trying to do, he called back immediately. I remember his cheery voice on my answering machine: 'Niklas Frank here, interesting project, very happy to help, any time . . .' A mellow, friendly voice with a south German burr. It could only be described as the voice of a balanced and happy man. Could he be the same man as the raving maniac who had written that furious book? Could he possibly have written himself free, freed himself of the horror of it all? Was this someone who had finally discovered a way of burning off the stinking heap of garbage behind his house, once and for all? Maybe it was as simple as that. Or so I thought.

In the Italian restaurant Niklas tells me that he wrote the book on a dope-fuelled binge that lasted twelve weeks. It was freezing outside, winter. Inside too: he sat at home in his bedroom in Eimsbüttel in his cap and overcoat. The little Erika typewriter he wrote on had belonged to his mother.

Why did he have to be so cold while he was writing? Why hadn't he turned the heating on? He doesn't go into this, says only that he and his wife never heated the bedroom. Every evening when he had finished writing, he would say the same phrase out loud to himself before going to sleep: 'Another day of blows struck against your father', meaning in the purely mechanical sense his hammering on the old keyboard, as well as in the symbolic one.

Another day of blows against the man who liked to call himself 'King of Poland', against the man who made Auschwitz possible, who has millions of dead to his name. I've written this more than once: the murderer Hans Frank, incarnation of evil. In the opening chapter and again later. I'm repeating myself. Why do I write it again here? Is there something about the dimensions of this barbarity that means I need go on reminding myself of them?

On page 8 of his book Niklas Frank hammered out these words:

> As a child I made your death my own. In particular, the nights of 16 October were sacred to me. I willed your death. I used to lie down naked on the stinking linoleum of the toilet, legs spread out, my left hand around my limp penis, and with a gentle rubbing movement I began to see you walking up and down in your cell, your fists pressed to your eyeballs, moaning to yourself for the hundredth time stupid soldiers' regulations about facing death with dignity, sitting down again and straining your ears to hear whether they're coming for you, you recognise the slightest sound because you've sat so long in your barred cell, your pulse is racing, you force yourself to read over your last letters to your loved ones at home, noticing perhaps how hollow and false and hypocritical they sound . . .
>
> [On page 17:] After the war, Mother liked to sit with the register of members of the Academy of German Law on her lap and to take a gloating

pleasure in ticking off the names she had come across, either in those big obituary spreads in the newspapers or in the announcement of appointments to the upper levels of the judiciary or public office. In Mother's register you could read a kind of national curriculum vitae, rather different from the one we now have in the age of the Federal Republic; in addition to which she knew many of them personally: 'Him? There was no bowing and scraping low enough for him!' Just imagine if you had survived, you, the archetypal all-time German criminal . . . of course you never personally murdered anyone with your own hands, but you ensured that it happened, exactly according to instructions. With a past life like yours you'd have fitted in well in the new Germany, a spot of gentle denazification and you'd have made the transition effortlessly from Nazis to CDU.[1]

[On pages 21 and 22:] What did I have of yours before I set off in search of you? A stamp that, when pressed onto a sheet of paper, replicates the resonant and telling words 'Property of the *Reichsminister* Dr Hans Frank' . . . Your prayer book too, which I have still, the thin little book in which you wrote me a last greeting the evening before you cried out: 'Jesus, have mercy.' A dedication that filled me with anger

---

[1] The *Christlich-Demokratische Union* or Christian Democratic Union.

because you wrote my name as 'Nicklas'. You don't make that mistake, I thought, not even in the hour of death.'

[On page 27:] How does a person like you come into being? I fish out your diary from the filth of your life . . .

[On page 45:] Why do I drag you through the mud like this? It gives me such a rebellious feeling. I'm still a young man . . . You're buried deep in my brain but some time, maybe when I'm an old man, I'll get hold of you, I'll get over you, and the noise of your neck breaking will grow fainter in my head.

[On page 62:] Come, Father, let's go on, the two of us, let me pluck your crown to pieces . . .

[On page 77:] For years, with Roland Freisler, you published the weekly *German Law Gazette* – that was one of my earliest encounters with you after a youth spent without you. I sat in a law seminar in Munich and read the forewords you'd written at the start of each of those thick red volumes. The more I read, the more anxious I became lest the other students would see that I was reading your text and that I was your son, so ghastly did I find your words about the new and mighty legal system for the German race, for the Germans and against the liberal, Jew-contaminated Roman law.

[And Niklas also wrote, on page 104:] I was allowed to go too, escorted by our nanny H. I didn't sit but stood in the back of the Mercedes, my nose pressed against the glass; there were black uniforms everywhere. We drove slowly along narrow streets, past skinny people in flapping clothes and children who stared at me with goggle eyes; it must have been a Sunday because I had my fetching little Pepita jacket and shorts on. Mummy, why aren't they smiling, why are they looking so cross, it's Sunday, Mummy, after all, and they've got such beautiful stars on their arms, and the – the men over there, the ones with whips. Goodness, child, you wouldn't understand, look, we're going shopping. There, on the corner, stop please, driver, their corselettes are rather good – oh yes, and the fur shop first. I stayed in the car and stuck my tongue out at another child. He went away, and I was the winner. I laughed but my nanny, my beloved H., dragged me away to one side; she sat silently and so did the driver as they waited for Mummy. Once I was allowed to get out of the car, as a reward for waiting like a good boy. A house with bars on windows and doors, a gloomy corridor, an arm lifts me up before a thick door, I'm supposed to peer through a small opening. 'There's a wicked, wicked witch sitting in there!' says the man. I see a woman, she sits with her back to the wall, she doesn't look up, she stares fixedly at the floor. I start to cry. 'She won't hurt you, she'll soon be dead,' the man comforts me.

Yes. Your ghettos, Father, they were really something. But I enjoyed another excursion more, the one to a camp with lots of huts and plenty of barbed wire around it, some kind of annexe to a concentration camp as I now know, but at the time it was just a hearty chap in uniform who had a wild donkey on which – how shrill my laughter sounded – thin men were mounted by powerful German hands, and the donkey bucked, and the men fell off, and they could only pick themselves up very slowly, and they didn't find it as funny as I did, they were put back on the donkey again and again, they helped each other, and the donkey got a good slap on the flank; it was a fantastic afternoon, and inside afterwards there was cocoa with the most important soldier.

These are the shitty images I carry around with me, Father . . .

At the restaurant Niklas Frank asks straightaway what we are going to do about the bill. He'll let me pay only if I am going to be reimbursed by my publisher. 'You're still young, you can use your money to get something started,' he says, 'whereas I'm an old fart with my life behind me.' Twenty years working for *Stern*, and what did he have to show for it? Sure, there was money. 'And apart from money?' 'Nothing, absolutely nothing.' He laughs, amused by the situation: like a siren announcing that the world is the very devil's brood. He chuckles again as he says, 'You know, I noticed fairly early on in my life that I radiate bad vibes. Not many people find me genuinely likeable.'

Niklas tells the story of his sister Brigitte, who died when she was forty-six. The family has always assumed it was suicide. She used to say she never wanted to grow any older than her father. 'She was obsessed by the idea.' Hans Frank was forty-six when he was hanged at Nuremberg.

He tells the story of his brother Michael. Michael died when he was fifty-three. 'He was such a handsome boy,' Niklas says and grins, 'a proper Adonis.' Politically he was to the right, far to the right, refusing to hear any criticism of his father, instead becoming heavily involved with the NPD. Then he started drinking. Not alcohol, however – milk. More than ten litres a day; at first all that happened was that he got fatter and fatter. 'My God, he was fat! He weighed two hundred kilos at the end. The doctor warned him: 'You can't go on like this, Herr Frank.' But he kept pouring those torrents of milk into himself and then he died because his organs couldn't cope any more.'

Both of them, sister and brother, died of their father, according to Niklas. It was obvious. 'None of us will ever be free of him.'

Norman, his elder brother, is still alive. 'We don't have to be together for more than two minutes before we start talking about our father.' He says that he loves his brother. 'Norman suffers worse than I do.' His brother knew his father for longer, and has good memories of him along with the bad. 'He still feels love for him, I think.' In an interview with the American journalist Gerald Posner at the end of the 1980s, Norman Frank said that he didn't want to have any children because he thought 'the name of Frank should bid this world farewell'.

Niklas Frank is a powerful presence, a man of substantial energy, which is something else that makes him seem weird. The truth is, he is a man who has had to endure a great deal. Knowing that his childhood, his life growing up as a boy after the war, was paid for with the royalties from his father's book *In the Gallows' Gaze*. (A book that became an underground bestseller in postwar Germany, selling more than 50,000 copies.) Knowing that his mother regularly received sympathetic letters from people at every level of German society who only wished her to know how much they had respected and admired her husband. No word of a lie: such were the exact words used by many, many Germans who wrote to the Frank household.

And he endured the letters he himself received when he published his series: letters that were filled with hate because no son should treat his father the way he had.

I find myself asking where exactly he lives, Niklas Frank, in what country? He has tried to conquer the past according to his own particular method, forcing his way in, direct, ruthless, self-lacerating, based on the principle of hate. I don't greatly care to use the word, but if ever the description 'honest' fitted, it fits the method Niklas Frank has chosen. He says he feels a great deal of his father in himself, his cowardice above all. He says too that there's a kind of freedom to be gained from looking so deep into the abyss: what more can happen to you there?

We go back briefly to his office at *Stern*. I ask him if he can spare me a copy of his book, because you can't get hold of it, it's been out of print for a long time. Which is a pity, because it is a big and important book; later maybe people will be astonished at how it was received in 1980s Germany.

In his small office there are two photos on the wall. One is a copy of a letter written by the Munich priest Rupert Mayer, who says that as soon as he gets out of the concentration camp, he will begin again to fight the Nazis. The other shows a fat Nazi threatening a young boy with a stick and forcing him to write the word 'Jew' on a wall. Niklas Frank says there isn't a single day 'when I don't find myself thinking of my father'.

He speaks of the anniversaries of his father's death, and of his masturbating back then as he thought about his father. He can only laugh, he says, when he thinks about how it upset people. 'Everybody thought Henry Miller was really great, then all of a sudden they say it's gone too far.' A fellow journalist, female and Jewish, had phoned him once on the subject and told him that she thought his masturbating on the anniversary of his father's death had been a way of challenging his father's death with his own lust for life. 'I was immediately convinced by that.'

Niklas Frank says he often dreams, even today, of the piles of corpses in the camps. He says his country will never be rid of that history, never. It was too appalling. 'It's a story that still is not over.'

At some point I leave. We've sat together for three hours. I need to get some fresh air along the waterfront. I need to think about the last pages of Niklas's book, where he imagines in a bloody orgy how the arm of God reaches deep into his father's body and turns him inside out. These are the final sentences:

> . . . and your heart strikes my face and I open my mouth and I bite into it, into your heart, and I feel you screaming and screaming – I bite hard, until it stops pumping and goes limp and you, in the witness box, hideous slab of flesh, collapse in a heap, while I, an eternally youthful zombie, spring from your body, again and again and again.

I walk along the Hamburg waterfront and I feel myself filling up with an anguish that oppresses me. I must have caught a bit too much Hell today.

The 1959 Manuscript:

GUDRUN HIMMLER

'HOW DO YOU imagine doing it?'

'I know it'll be a difficult job,' Gudrun Himmler replies.

'Don't you think it might be impossible?'

'No.'

Gudrun Himmler is thirty years old, a woman outwardly the same as thousands of others. She works as a secretary, lives in a small flat, goes out to the theatre and parties and *Fasching*.[1] But unlike the others she wants something else at the same time: to be the one person on this earth who can rehabilitate Heinrich Himmler.

'When did you see your father for the last time?'

'In November 1944 he came to Gmund for a couple of days. After that we only managed to phone each other, which we did very often.'

'Right till the end?'

---

[1] The German Shrovetide carnival.

'Yes, more or less. Though obviously we didn't discuss the political situation. Actually, we usually talked about my problems.'

At fourteen, the girl was deeply attached to her father. She cut out every picture of him from the newspapers and glued them into a large scrapbook. She embroidered and made little handicrafts and wood carvings for him.

'In those days', I say to her, 'you saw things from a child's perspective. Today you've grown up, and you know that your childhood memories can't possibly be the whole truth. If you want to stand up for your father, you have to get to grips with his life, with his views, with the orders he gave.'

'I'm aware of that,' Gudrun replies. 'The documents are in America, and I don't yet have the money to travel there. But I will . . .'

'And from the chance to study those documents from his time as *Reichsführer-SS* and chief of police – you're promising yourself results?'

'Yes. My intuition tells me yes. Unfortunately, the official German material that's available is very limited. And my father's closest colleagues are either dead or – for reasons I understand very well – don't want to be reminded of that time any more.'

In ten or twenty years' time, she believes, she will be in a position to write a book called simply *Heinrich Himmler*. By her reckoning it will take her that long to gather together the material she needs to clear her father's name. She plans to devote one chapter to his suicide, because she doubts it was suicide.

The *Reichsführer-SS* and family. (Bilderdienst Süddeutscher Verlag)

'I don't believe he swallowed that poison capsule,' she says. 'My mother and I have never had official notification of his death. It wasn't even until 1947 that his death was entered in the Lüneburg District Court register . . .'

Heinrich Himmler's corpse was cremated on Lüneburg Heath. His ashes were scattered to the four winds. The body was photographed beforehand, and the pictures published.

'In those pictures', his daughter declares today, 'he looks more as though he was about to inspect a parade. He had a typical way of placing his hands on those occasions, and I don't accept that he'd hold his hands that way if, as it was reported, he was biting into a poison capsule. I believe that picture shows him really inspecting a parade. To me it's a retouched photo from when he was alive.'

'What do you suppose happened?' I ask.

'I don't suppose anything. I only want to carry out more research. Nothing more has ever been heard of the British soldiers who are supposed to have been present when my father committed suicide. The last time he was seen for certain was by some SS personnel at Colkhagen prisoner-of-war camp, from where he was fetched at six in the morning by some soldiers in a Jeep.'

Whatever really happened on Lüneburg Heath, even his daughter is in no doubt about one thing: Heinrich Himmler is dead.

Himmler too could only have expected the gallows at Nuremberg. Yet at a time when his name was cursed in Germany like no other, a teenage girl persisted doggedly in upholding it. For Gudrun, he was still her father, and she would endure prisons and camps on his account. She chose a rocky path for herself . . .

She hung on grimly to her father: she vowed herself to him. She did not weep, but went on hunger strike. She lost weight, fell sick, stopped developing. She couldn't pray and she no longer smiled. The British officer in charge of her care was heard to say, 'What in God's name am I to do with this child?'

In the late spring of 1945 General Wolff was celebrating his birthday at the royal villa at Bolzano, Italy. In the grounds roses bloomed, children played and German soldiers bivouacked.

In the main reception room German officers bowed to the general, *Sekt* glasses in hand. Only one had no part to play in the celebrations: an *SS-Hauptsturmführer* under arrest and currently in detention in one of the attic rooms.

In the villa's many corridors sumptuous floral arrangements burst forth. Canapés were served, and the guards saluted as they had in the best of times. The banqueting table was laid.

At midday the general was about to call his birthday guests in to lunch. Suddenly the idyll was disturbed as heavy American tanks came rolling over the roses in the park. White-helmeted American military police, their machine pistols drawn, rushed the villa and arrested its occupants, allowing only one to go free: the *SS-Hauptsturmführer* in the attic. It had been his great good fortune to fall into disgrace at the right moment, and he was able to watch as General Wolff was led away with his guests.

In return the *Hauptsturmführer* conveyed a useful tip to his liberators: the location to which the *Reichsführer-SS* had evacuated his wife and daughter.

Thus it was that on 13 May Gudrun Himmler saw a Jeep pull up in front of the Casa al Monte house on the Wolkenstein. She was just bringing up from the cellar a cashbox full of valuables she had hidden there. There was

no time to put it back. In any case, it was of no importance any more.

'*Mitkommen*,' an American sergeant ordered Frau
Marga Himmler.

'What about Gudrun?' the *Reichsführer*'s wife asked.

'*Auch mitkommen. Alle mitkommen.*'

The only person left behind was a young German plain-
clothes officer assigned to the Himmler family for their
protection, who had accompanied them to the Casa al
Monte. The Americans ignored him at first. Then, as the
Jeep drove off with his charges on board, the young man
gave the regulation salute: '*Heil Hitler!*' The American
sergeant slammed on the brakes, jumped down from the
Jeep and grabbed the bodyguard roughly by the shoulder.
'That's all over now, get used to it!'

It was indeed over. Mother and daughter Himmler were
locked in a room at the Post Hotel in Bolzano. Their hairpins, nail scissors, nail files and other sharp instruments
were taken away.

'Why?' Gudrun Himmler wanted to know.

'So you don't try to kill yourselves,' someone answered.

In the evening two American soldiers unlocked the
room and began laying the table. White damask table-
cloth, plates, bowls, cutlery, wine glasses . . .

'Sit down,' a GI ordered.

The Himmlers sat down at the table. As if at a signal,
two cameramen appeared, set up their lights and filmed
the scene.

'Just for the press,' the GI grinned, clearing the table
away again.

It was nevertheless the great good fortune of Marga Himmler and her daughter that it was only a couple of cameramen who were aware of who was enjoying an enforced stay at the Post Hotel.

In the streets of Bolzano those who had been partisans pelted German prisoners of war with rotten tomatoes. German officers were being spat at, Italian Fascists lynched. What mischief might the family of Heinrich Himmler have suffered?

That same night, the Himmlers were transferred to Verona. The streets had been torn up, the woods were ablaze. They remained twelve hours at a transit camp. Their next destination was a camp at Florence. During the day it was unbearably hot in the Quonset huts. The latrines stank. 'If you say your name is Himmler, you'll be torn apart,' a sentry told them helpfully.

Moved again, for twelve days they had rooms in a house with a roof garden. They were even allowed to go for a daily walk, and the food improved. The price of their comfort was that this was the start of their interrogation.

Gudrun found herself opposite a British officer of no great stature who lit one cigarette after another.

'Do you smoke?' he asked.

'No.'

'How old are you?'

'Fifteen.'

'Are you married?'

'I'm fifteen,' Gudrun repeated.

'So what?' snapped the officer, who spoke strikingly good German. 'How many children?'

'I'm fifteen,' Gudrun replied for the third time.

'When your name's Himmler, anything's possible,' said the officer.

When your name's Himmler – it was a phrase she would hear often. Later she became used to it, but at that first interrogation her lips trembled with anger. She thought of the villa by the Tegernsee, of school at Reichersbeuern, of everything she had left behind her.

'Where's my father?' she asked.

The British officer stood up and leaned forward a long way over his desk. For a moment it looked as though he would strike her, but he simply said in a trembling voice: 'Do you know how many people your father cremated at Dachau? Or how many he gassed at Oranienburg? Of course you do. You're Herr Himmler's daughter, after all.'

Gudrun was silent.

The interrogating officer exhaled sharply from his cigarette and also fell silent. For a while he looked out of the window, turning his back on her. When he sat again at his desk, he was calm.

'Have you ever been to a concentration camp?' he asked.

'Once, to Dachau,' she answered.

'With your father?'

'Yes.'

'And what did you see there?'

'My father showed me a herb garden and explained the different herbs to me.'

'I see.' The British officer drummed on the desk with yellow-stained fingers. 'You're asking me to believe you didn't see any prisoners?'

'I saw some prisoners,' said Gudrun.

'And what did your father explain to you about them?'

'That the ones with the red triangle were political prisoners and the others were criminals.'

The interrogation did not last much longer. Gudrun was returned to her mother. They resumed their journey south. Their next stop was Rome, where there was a camp located a long way outside the city, among the film studios of Cinecittà. Overnight the British had transformed the dressing rooms and props stores into cells for internees. Cinecittà in fact was no ordinary prison camp; it was the hub of British intelligence. Here were to be found Helferich, chief of the *Abwehr*; Klaus Hügel, German chief of the SD – security service – for Switzerland; General Wolff, arrested in Bolzano; *Generaloberst* von Wittinghoff; the Italian Prince Borghese and Marshal Graziani; rank-and-file soldiers; and suspected war criminals . . .

The sun beat down hard on the camp at Cinecittà. The tiny cells were like compartments of an oven that was lit punctually every morning. Prisoners crawled beneath their camp beds to find shade. The water ran warm from the taps.

Camp food was an indigestible plate of mushy peas twice a day. The sole entertainment was the camp spokesman, who appeared weekly. 'Pope Pius XII expressed himself in strong terms on the subject of

Nazism . . .', 'Yokohama, Japan's second most important port, has been as good as destroyed as a centre of production after last Tuesday's air raid . . .', 'Allied Headquarters has announced that two members of the Hitler Youth have been executed after being found guilty of spying . . .'

Heinrich Himmler's wife and daughter were the only female presence at Cinecittà.

After four weeks at the camp, Gudrun began a hunger strike in protest at the mushy peas. On the first day the guards laughed. On the second day they gazed doubtfully. On the third day they informed the intelligence officer in charge, Major Bridge.

Gudrun Himmler was too weak to raise herself from her bed. Her hands were hot and feverish.

'There are no other rations available,' the major tried to explain to her. 'If you don't want to eat what we give you, then you must go hungry. Our soldiers who are fighting the Japanese don't have anything better.'

Gudrun Himmler continued to refuse all nourishment.

On the evening of the fourth day Major Bridge strode into the cell of the Himmlers' neighbour, Dr Eugen Dollmann, the man who had interpreted between Hitler and Mussolini.

'Do you know Gudrun Himmler?'

'Yes.'

'Can't you get her to see sense and start eating again? She's going to die on us otherwise.'

'Give her something decent to eat,' said Dr Dollmann, 'and she'll soon eat.'

'I can't make any exceptions,' said the Major.

'And you'd let a child die for that?' asked Dollmann.

Major Bridge shook his head ill-humouredly. 'What am I supposed to do with her?'

Gudrun won her hunger strike, achieving officer's rations for herself and her mother. On the other front she accomplished nothing: try as she might, she could elicit no word about her father's fate.

Until 20 August 1945.

On that day an American journalist came to interview *Reichsführer* Himmler's wife in her cell. Gudrun and a British officer sat silently with her.

The reporter asked the usual questions. Where did you meet your husband? What was he like at home? Did he enjoy staying home and wearing slippers? What do you know about the camps?

Suddenly, between questions, Gudrun asked him: 'Where's my father now?'

'He's dead,' replied the reporter. 'He poisoned himself a while back.'

The stunned silence that greeted his answer was broken by the British officer. 'You weren't authorised to say that.'

'I'm sorry,' the American apologised.

He had not been authorised to say it, but now Gudrun knew. The consequences were immediate. The fifteen-year-old suffered a psychological and medical breakdown. Shivering, running a temperature of forty degrees celsius, day and night she lay delirious on the bed in her cell. It seemed by no means certain that the medical staff would be able to nurse her back to health.

One day three weeks later she was able to get up from her bed once more. From that day forward, Major Bridge of British intelligence had a single aspiration: to pass the uncomfortable Himmlers on to some other party as rapidly as possible.

But who and where?

Who in September 1945 would have wanted to take on a woman and a girl by the name of Himmler? No one. Not even a camp.

The major eventually solved the problem by having papers made out in the name of Schmidt, after which he had Frau and Fräulein Schmidt swiftly bundled off to Florence by military transport.

From Florence the two were shipped on to Milan. Lacking a suitable camp, the authorities quartered mother and daughter in a prison. 'The prison was overcrowded,' Gudrun Himmler remembers. 'Almost entirely women and children. As it very quickly became clear, they were fanatical fascists. They sang the "Giovinezza", the fascist anthem, for nights on end. The prison officers were communist ex-partisans, and the women were forever being thrashed, but despite the beatings they went on singing. There was no question of anyone sleeping.'

One morning Frau and Fräulein Schmidt were fetched by an American major and driven to the airport.

'Where's the plane going?' they asked.

'Paris.'

'Then my name's Himmler again,' said Gudrun decisively.

'Schmidt would still be safer,' the major pointed out.

'I don't care. My name is Gudrun Himmler.'

They changed planes at Marseille and in the afternoon landed at Paris-Orly. That evening they went to sleep, dog-tired, in a bathroom at Versailles. Under guard, obviously, since this villa too was temporarily doing service as a prison. Diplomats occupied some of the rooms; the guards were American. The food was good.

But the bathroom at Versailles was just another episode. After three days there, the Himmlers heard the familiar command: '*Mitkommen!*'

'Where are we going this time?'

'No idea,' the American grunted.

A car. A plane swapped for another plane. And at the journey's end another vehicle waiting at the airfield: green with barred windows.

Gudrun looked around her. 'Where are we now?'

And someone said: 'Nuremberg.'

'No talking!' roared a German auxiliary policeman.

The green police van pulled up half an hour later in front of Nuremberg's Palace of Justice, where in three weeks' time the trial of the twenty-one principal war-crimes defendants was to begin.

The door was opened, and Gudrun and Marga Himmler stepped down.

Gudrun was separated from her mother immediately. A ginger-haired American master sergeant led the pale girl with the thin blonde plaits to a cell and said casually, 'Get undressed.'

'Undressed . . . here?'

'Get undressed. We don't have all day.'

'Please go outside and close the door,' Gudrun asked.

But the door stayed open. Modesty had little place at Nuremberg prison. The guards had strict orders not to let the prisoners out of their sight, so they didn't let them out of their sight. Every opportunity for a suicide attempt was to be prevented. The ginger-haired master sergeant made sure that Gudrun was relieved of all sharp objects, that her shoelaces were removed from her shoes and the elastic from her knickers.

The precautions were justified, though they failed to hinder all ingenuity. The former chief of the Reich's health department, Dr Leonardo Conti, tore himself free from his guards and threw himself into the stairwell.[2] He died immediately. And Robert Ley[3] knotted together a sling from the zip-fastener of his army jacket and hanged himself from the lever of the WC in his cell.

Gudrun Himmler was allowed to put her clothes back on. The master sergeant handed her over to a military policeman as tall as a telegraph pole. All MPs at the Palace of Justice were as tall as telegraph poles, wore white gloves and carried white truncheons that looked like marshal's batons.

They climbed three steps, turning into a long, broad

---

[2] Other accounts state that Dr Conti committed suicide in his cell by fastening a towel around his neck and jumping from his chair.

[3] The former Reich organiser of the German Labour Front and initiator of the Werewolf partisan organisation at the end of the war.

corridor. Neon bathed them in a lurid white light. The cells on either side resembled the counters in a post office. Instead of the peepholes customary in prisons, these cells had hinged shutters, all in the 'up' position. Above them names were painted in large letters: Rudolf Hess, Joachim von Ribbentrop, Julius Streicher, Ernst Kaltenbrunner – no mere post-office officials.

Shocked, Gudrun stopped in front of the first counter. On the other side of the hatch Hermann Göring could be seen, looking strangely bald and old. Gudrun stared at him. Göring seemed to stop and think for a moment, then laughed quietly as he recognised the young girl on the other side of the door.

She wanted to wave. But the MP shoved her forward. 'Go on.'

Soon afterwards she found the door closing on her own cell, with her own hinged shutter and WC. The first night she was alone, though not abandoned, for every half-hour, sometimes more often, a white helmet and a pair of eyes would appear at the hatch and an MP's gaze would check that all was well with Himmler's daughter. She noticed that the eyes were blue to begin with, then dark brown, then green. The guards were relieved frequently.

The night beneath the neon light on the ceiling passed slowly. Gudrun was unable to sleep. The only reading matter she had was the 'House Rules for Prisoners' written by Major Elmer W. Fox.

Internees are forbidden to speak to each other. In no

case must they attempt to enter into communication with each other or other persons . . .

No internee may attempt to escape. In the event of attempted escape they will be struck down or shot down. It is their fault if they are wounded in the process . . .

Internees may take a shower-bath once a week . . .

Every internee will be given a Bible on request . . .

Internees will be conducted to exercise daily . . . They are forbidden to approach each other closer than a distance of 10 metres . . .

Since exchange of military salutes between prisoners and members of the Allied forces is forbidden, the customary form of greeting of a bow is regarded as a suitable substitute for intercourse between internees and Allied officers . . .

The following day Gudrun was placed with her mother in a double cell containing two plank beds and two WCs. An American spent some time carefully painting the name Himmler over the hatch outside.

Nothing else happened before the trial. In accordance with the rules, each day mother and daughter were taken via a winding staircase to stretch their legs in the prison yard. On one occasion Gudrun was collected by the guards and taken for questioning. Like all the others, she was asked to make a statement on oath, and her statement was recorded on tape. The questioning was brief and unproductive. She had nothing to say about concentration camps, the persecution of the Jews, the SS or the

Gestapo. There were no revelations that she could contribute. The only phenomenon she was able to describe was Herr Himmler at home.

'How often did you see Hitler?' asked the interrogating officer finally.

'I really can't remember any more.'

'Did you ever receive any gifts from him?'

'Yes,' Gudrun replied. 'On 24 December I used to drive with my father to see him at the Brown House in Munich and wish him merry Christmas.'

'And?'

'When I was little he used to give me dolls. Later on he always gave me a box of chocolates.'

At Christmas 1945 the outlook was somewhat different. It was a meagre and sad Christmas for all, for the Germans at liberty as much as for those still held in camps and prisons. Outside or in, they had nothing to eat, nothing to wear and nothing to laugh about.

Gudrun was moved next with her mother to the so-called witnesses' wing at Nuremberg. The regulations governing witnesses were slightly more relaxed. During the day, female inmates were even allowed to visit one another. For the most part they were secretaries – the 'right hands' of Hitler, Hess, Ribbentrop, Ley, Frank and other top Nazis. They were awaiting their turn in the witness stand in the main trial, which had begun on 20 November.

Why the fifteen-year-old Gudrun was being kept with them, no one knew. She was granted the odd privilege: she was occasionally allowed, for example, to use the gymnasium. She was permitted to borrow books from the library. She was given exercise books to write in, coloured crayons, silver paper. She had to be kept occupied. So while the prison buzzed with a permanent coming and going – some prisoners had been called before the Military Tribunal, others were being fetched for interrogation, still others had only just arrived – Heinrich Himmler's daughter was cutting out little snowmen from silver paper, gluing them with Christmas stars, and dropping them into the prison letterboxes. Believe it or not, many of her little silver-paper snowmen found their way to other prisoners' cells. Later, they were grateful for her kindness.

'*Mitkommen!*' It was 6 January 1946.

'Where to?'

The military policeman grinned. He didn't know either. He handed mother and daughter their shoelaces, hairpins and knicker elastic and asked them to sign a receipt.

'Goodbye,' he said and grinned. It was always a good idea to grin.

Their next stop was an internment camp at Hersbruck. The one following that was an internment camp at Ludwigsburg. Gudrun and Marga Himmler gradually accustomed themselves to their new way of life. They also began to realise that it was likely to be better for them to live behind barbed wire than to go out into the world bearing the name of Himmler.

They had in any case lost all touch with the world around them, all contact with former friends and acquaintances. They received not a single letter or parcel. Nor, naturally, any visitors.

They were not, however, allowed to be bored in the 77th Ludwigsburg internment camp.

'We could learn English, child care, stenography and needlework,' Gudrun remembers. 'There was a revue, there were lectures on gardening and history, and drawing lessons. I remember trying my hand at book-binding . . .'

She was still pale and thin and wore plaits. People took her for twelve, though by now she was already sixteen. During a lecture about the young Goethe, she fainted and fell from her chair. When she woke six hours later, she

Frau Himmler with her daughter at the staged dinner given by the Americans at the Post Hotel, Bolzano, shortly after their capture. (Bilderdienst Süddeutscher Verlag)

found herself in hospital. She was discharged a couple of days later but her doctor made a telephone call to the camp authorities. 'The patient is nine kilos underweight. She could have another fainting attack at any time.'

After the hospital's phone call Gudrun was given supplementary rations, but her fainting attacks recurred.

In November 1946 Frau Himmler was summoned by the camp authorities.

'You're to be released,' the camp superintendent informed her. 'Where would you like us to make out the release form for?'

'I don't know,' the widow of the once mighty *Reichsführer* replied.

'Don't you have any relations, acquaintances or friends you could go and stay with for a while?'

'No,' said Marga Himmler.

'Do you have any money?'

'None.'

'No jewellery or items of value you could sell?' asked the superintendent.

'Nothing.'

The Ludwigsburg camp superintendent shook his head. 'Then the best thing you can do is go back to your hut. I can't just put you and your daughter out on the street.'

But he knew he could not hold the two of them at the camp either: after all, it was not a hostel for the homeless. So a week later he drew a sigh of relief when he was at last able to make out a release form for a place named Bethel, near Bielefeld.

The Protestant nursing home at Bethel had been founded a hundred years before by a pastor Bodelschwingh. Over the years it had grown to the size of a small town – according to the wishes of its founder, a town for 'those in physical and spiritual need'. It had 2,500 epileptics, 800 mentally ill patients, women rescued from the streets, and socially dysfunctional and homeless people living there by the time Gudrun and her mother moved into two small rooms in a house named Damascus.

'We were fed and given a roof over our heads,' Gudrun says today. 'At the time, in November 1946, it was undoubtedly a stroke of good fortune for us. Who else would have taken us in?'

Among the physically and spiritually needy of Bethel, the sixteen-year-old nevertheless refused to take the home's evangelical beliefs into her heart. She refused to go to church on Sundays and during midday and evening prayers she kept silent. 'I want to stay the way my father was,' she repeated stubbornly to the pastors and sisters who strove to reclaim her soul.

In the devout atmosphere of Bethel, Gudrun remained an outsider. She learned to spin and weave. But she didn't learn in order to be able to fit in. She made no friends there, but remained almost a child, a lonely, rebellious, unloved child who never prayed and whom no one ever saw laugh or cry.

In the autumn of 1947 she travelled to Bielefeld and applied for admission to the town's fashion and design school.

Frau Marga Himmler and Gudrun at the time of their
detention as witnesses at Nuremberg. (Timepix)

'What's your name?'

'Gudrun Himmler.'

'Your father's profession?'

'My father was the *Reichsführer-SS* . . .'

Her application was turned down by return. The fact
that she was nevertheless able to enrol for the autumn
term was thanks to the SPD chairman for Bielefeld, who
offered to meet her in his office for a talk.

'You're Himmler's daughter?'

'Yes.'

'It's not something you can do anything about . . .'

'But that's the reason my application was turned down.'

'I'll make sure you get your place in our school, don't worry. In the new Germany we don't have guilt by family association.'

'Thank you,' said Gudrun. And the gentleman who had thus provided her with her first lesson in practical democracy kept his word.

Until the time of the currency reform, she attended textile classes at the design school. Subsequently she had to drop out, because she was no longer able to pay her tuition fees. Her application for a scholarship was turned down on the grounds that the taxpayer could not be expected to finance the studies of Heinrich Himmler's daughter.

So Gudrun became apprenticed to a dressmaker. In 1951 she passed her journeyman's examination. In the same year she received her denazification notice: 'You cannot expiate your father's crimes, but you have an obligation to live a life worthy of a German citizen and to live honestly and decently.'

A year later she left her mother. She packed her suitcase in Bethel and travelled to Munich. She was now twenty-two and finally looked her age. She began to go to the cinema and theatre. In Bielefeld she had not only learned dressmaking, but had also learned to dance.

'I began the process of waking up there,' she says now about her years in Bielefeld.

'Did you get to know any young men there too?'

'Yes . . . of course.'

'The name of Himmler wasn't a problem then?'

'No.'

But in Munich the name of Himmler became a problem when she began to look for work. At the clothing factory where she first presented herself, the works committee called a meeting. The vote went against Fräulein Himmler, and the personnel department was forced to turn her down.

Then she had as good as been taken on by the boss of a fashion house when the woman suddenly asked: 'And of course, dear child, you're nothing to do with that dreadful Himmler, are you?'

'I'm his daughter,' said Gudrun, and with the admission lost that job too.

'If you were to take another name, you could start with me tomorrow,' she was told by one couturier.

'No, thank you.'

'Then why not get married, for form's sake?' he suggested.

'No, thank you.'

'Then I'm sorry. I'm afraid I have my customers' feelings to consider.'

A string of refusals later, she finally succeeded in finding work as a cutter, and a room of her own. And finally made her first trip to England.

'I got to know many fascists there,' she remembers. For example, a certain Mr Sidney Proud, who invited her and Adolf von Ribbentrop, the son of the hanged foreign minister, to his house and proudly showed off the portraits of Hitler that hung over his fireplace. He served them German *Sekt* and sang the Horst-Wessel song. He had also arranged for a photographer to be present.

The pictures of Sidney Proud's party appeared in newspapers all over the world. They had two very different consequences. For Proud, whose main employment was arranging trips to France and Spain, they were cheap publicity. For Gudrun Himmler and Adolf von Ribbentrop they were a terrible embarrassment, because they roused people's ire everywhere against the apparently incorrigible Nazi children. Directly after her trip to England, Gudrun lost her first job with a resounding crash, before she had even really started.

One Monday, she started her second job punctually at eight a.m. in the office of a private hotel on the Tegernsee.

At eleven o'clock, as previously announced, Dr Goldmann arrived from Frankfurt. He intended to stay for three weeks. Gudrun handed him the key to room number seven.

Dr Goldmann had white hair and was in his seventies. After lunch he made two long-distance calls. Gudrun connected him: 'Just a moment, I'm putting you through now to Herr Dr Goldmann.'

Until four in the afternoon all was well between Gudrun and the white-haired Dr Goldmann. Then he learned from someone who the girl in the office downstairs was.

Gudrun heard him raging as he stormed downstairs. 'I once had a wife who was murdered at Auschwitz. Am I supposed to thank Fräulein Himmler for that?'

Two hours later Heinrich Himmler's daughter was standing on the platform at Gmund station, waiting for the next train to Munich. She was unemployed again.

Once again she would have to start from scratch, introduce herself, say her name, her father's name . . .

She became a cutter, a piece-worker, an office assistant and finally a secretary. She changed jobs often, moving from one rented room to the next; she changed her hairstyle and, with time, her personality. Only one thing has not changed: wherever she presents herself, wherever she surfaces, the question always comes with deadly certainty.

'Himmler? You wouldn't by any chance be related to . . . ?'

An Embittered Daughter and the Not-Wanting-to-See Principle

SUPPOSE MY FATHER had been one of the perpetrators, and I had one day learned what he had done. I'd have known immediately that I had a criminal for a father, a murderer. It would be of no consequence whether he had issued the fatal orders sitting at his desk, or whether he had done the killing with his bare hands.

I would still have had the same pictures of him in my head as the ones I have today. The 'good pictures', so to speak, of which there are more than enough. Of how he used to play Tip-Kick with his boys at lunchtime, lying on the floor next to the green plastic pitch. He was particularly proud of a tricky move he had developed with the die-cast miniature footballers, the 'special shot' as he called it.

I would remember just as clearly how he was always there when a problem cropped up. That he always had time for us, whether we were going fishing (and not once did we ever bring a fish home with us) or playing cards (he insisted early on that we should play for real money, because nothing else was real). That he often took us to the railway station whenever he had a manuscript to post at the post office next door. We used to eat *Leberkäse*, a Bavarian speciality, at one of the fast-food stands, and today, whenever I find myself at a station, I can still taste it in my mouth.

There are many such memories. I can still remember the time when I first turned up at the editorial offices of the *Süddeutsche Zeitung* – the same newspaper my father had worked for many years before – and found myself in the office of the crime reporter. Seeing me, he immediately said: 'You must be related to the Lebert who used to work here, you've got his smile.' It felt strange to hear this. I thought: Apparently the bonds between us are stronger than I'd supposed. They must be, if strangers are telling me how alike we are. So does the feeling of being a son have something to do with the question of what portion of me is derived from my father and what portion is me alone?

I could make it easy on myself and say that the way my father was, with all his qualities, made it impossible for him to perpetrate violence. But isn't that exactly the reasoning so many Germans used at the end of the Second World War? The thinking that went: I know my father, my brother, my friend, my husband, they would never do such a thing. They knew nothing, they can't have known anything. And if they did know something, they must have been led astray by the real devils, the few who really knew. No, this was no land of evildoers.

Look us in the face: we too are human beings, we too were victims.

The Nazi hunter Simon Wiesenthal says that it is a grave and dramatic mistake to proceed on the basis that only evil beings are capable of evil acts. One of the essential characteristics of many leading National Socialists, says Wiesenthal, was that at home they were utterly charming people. 'They were the same people who lovingly kissed their children goodbye in the mornings and then a few hours later were gassing or shooting Jews.' This realisation, Wiesenthal thinks, is dreadful and at the same time hugely important, 'because only the person who has grasped it knows that evil lies dormant in most people and can break out at almost any time. Let no man say that such a ghastly dictatorship is no longer possible today. That is the true lesson from the horror of National Socialism: we must fight against it constantly, against evil, so that it does not emerge again.'

In fact my father's biography came pretty close to being that of a perpetrator. I've already mentioned how, as an enthusiastic Hitler Youth, he would stick little flags into his map of the world, in the many countries successfully overrun by Hitler at the beginning of the war. The collapse of Nazi Germany, he said, was a catastrophe for him: he experienced the Allied occupation not as a liberation but as a great defeat. He used to say he despised the people who stood in the streets and waved to the Americans. To him they were traitors.

When the war was brought to an end, my father was

fifteen. One should make allowance for the fact that he was still a boy. He saw it that way too. 'I had the good fortune not to have been any older, that spared me dreadful things.' He meant not only war, which he felt he continued to be spared, but above all the possibility of becoming a leading Nazi, with all the consequences that that would have meant. 'My God, what kind of a person would I have become if we Germans hadn't lost the war?' Perhaps a *Gauleiter* named Norbert Lebert, somewhere in the great National Socialist Reich. He was quite clear about this. 'Given my unconditional enthusiasm at the time, there's no reason to assume that things would have turned out any other way.'

Until the day he died he was imbued with, and haunted by, the realisation that one cannot trust oneself, that one is capable of anything, even the most wicked acts, when external circumstances call them forth. The only thing that didn't chime with this lifelong burden was that he also thought of himself as one who had been led astray. He knew one thing, which was that one should take good care never to treat one's own moral code as something universally valid.

When he finally grasped what had happened, when he saw the pictures from the camps, of the mountains of corpses and the emaciated faces of starving prisoners, he reacted in a manner that one can see as representative, up to a point, of a great number of Germans. He resolved that until further notice he would have nothing to do with politics, or with any attempts to deal with the past, and that he would instead devote himself to his private life and his own career. Put it another way: pleasure and money were the order of the day, and no looking back under any circumstances. A pattern that without a doubt came to typify and embody the Federal Republic's fifty years of existence.

And if he had been one of the perpetrators? I think, I hope, I would have had the strength to break with him. In whatever way I could. Though I'm nowhere near sure of myself. I have a hunch about how much there is left inside, about the pictures that vie for attention in one's memory. If nothing else, I'm aware of the burden that remains.

How exactly do you feel when someone remarks on your great resemblance to your father, if your father was a mass murderer? I imagine the emotional conflict rather along the lines of Carol Reed's film *The Third Man*. The story has an American writer newly arrived in the ruins of postwar Vienna with the purpose of visiting his old friend Harry Lime. He learns that his friend has become a ruthless racketeer who dilutes life-saving drugs such as penicillin in order to increase his profits. In a memorable scene, the writer is taken by the military police to a hospital ward full of children stricken by the contaminated penicillin. The spectator sees the American's horrified expression but not the children, who are out of shot and represented only by a couple of cuddly toys. So this is his old friend, these are his deeds! The film's finale is well known: heavy of heart, the writer acts as bait for the police and eventually shoots Harry Lime in the Vienna sewers.

Obviously the atrocities of a Heinrich Himmler cannot be compared to the racketeering of a Harry Lime. I'm talking exclusively about the emotional conflict, about which we have heard so strangely little in the intervening decades. Yet in a land of perpetrators it must nevertheless have been a decisive element after the war, in the wake of the definitive realisation of what the Nazis had served up. Certainly there was the collective outcry of the '68ers: 'What did you do in the war?' But it remained a cry of demonstrators, the shout of individual students. It was a shout that failed to reach most German families even as a softly spoken, carefully phrased question. Apparently it was not mentioned.

Dan Bar-On wrote in his book *The Burden of Silence*:

. . . as part of my investigation I am on the lookout for 'confessional situations' involving Nazi perpetrators: did they ever go to priests (or doctors or psychologists) to own up to criminal acts in which they had participated during the war? During my first two stays in Germany I talked to approximately eighty priests, doctors, psychologists and psychiatrists, but not one of them could report a single instance of such a confession. Only one psychiatrist and one doctor had heard of colleagues who had experienced such a thing.

I should add that these researches of Bar-On's took place in the mid-1980s.

In the 1960s the Heidelberg psychologists Alexander

and Margarete Mitscherlich made the following statement about the psychological health of the Germans:

> Astonishingly [our experience] in no way points to the kind of increase in the number of patients in a state of denial that might have encouraged us to identify a tangibly clinical illness. From the records of more than 4,000 patients it emerges that extremely few criteria could be found for a correlation between their present-day symptoms and their experiences in the Nazi era. Self-confessed Nazis virtually never appeared.

The Freiburg psychoanalyst Tilmann Moser offered a similar conclusion at the end of the 1990s:

> It seems that we must resign ourselves to the fact that the perpetrators and their followers have uncovered no path to shame or guilt within themselves, and for this reason we remain faced with: cleavage, defiance, cognitive dysfunction, collective denial and anthropological limits to the establishment of identity and the continuity of conscience.

After countless studies, his Munich counterpart Wolfgang Schmidbauer has come to accept the 'intensely unjust' state of affairs that for the camp murderer who has killed over and over again, or the camp employer who has profited by the deaths of thousands of helpless slave labourers, it is far easier to deny guilt, to shrug off scruples, to live a normal family life and be a respected father to his children, than it is for the victims, who are mostly visited by the severest feelings of guilt because they are the ones who survived. You have to look at it this way, Schmidbauer concludes: the perpetrators had to deal only with their fear of being caught and condemned. From a psychological viewpoint, it comes down to understanding that the perpetrator realised him- or herself through his or her act, whereas the victim was hindered by the same act in everything that he wanted, and wants still, to realise. Or put it more cynically: torturing body and spirit has measurably fewer side effects than being tortured.

Among those who survived the Holocaust, one can often observe great restlessness and a tendency to excessive levels of work, Schmidbauer notes. Both qualities have something in common: such people are always in motion, never still, and never stop simply to reflect on who they are – such a thought is intolerable. And it is precisely for this reason that so many victims of the camps have a deeply problematic relationship with their children, 'because', says Schmidbauer, 'one has to stand still where children are concerned, one has to devote oneself to them. You have to make it clear to them who you are. Which is exactly what many with that shared past cannot do.' And what of the perpetrators? There are no known problems, he says. 'By far the greatest number are apparently perfectly at ease with themselves.'

In his 1998 book *I Never Knew What Was Wrong with My Father: War and Its Trauma*, Schmidbauer also looked for a synthesising picture of the various repercussions on successive generations.

> If a young woman visitor to the memorials at Auschwitz and Buchenwald – born in, say, 1959 – weeps plentiful tears and can't sleep for nightmares afterwards, she's probably the daughter of camp victims. And if the woman next to her takes in the scene with a tourist's interest and finally comes out with a few well-chosen phrases about how dreadful, unparalleled and unrepeatable the Holocaust is in a united Europe, then there's every chance that she's a daughter or niece of one of those responsible.

No path to shame or guilt: perhaps the phrase well describes the fifty-year existence of postwar Germany. People worked at reconstruction, amused themselves, enjoyed life after the long dark years. Many have testified to their surprise at how quickly everything got moving and started to improve again, 'we never expected it'.

My father described life in the 1950s as like being drunk all the time: the appetite for life was so vast, people wanted to absorb everything, the one thing they didn't want was to burden themselves with anything heavy. It was plainly selfish and, considered objectively, highly understandable. I'm sure I would have functioned exactly the same way.

Equally understandable is the view of Alan Dershowitz, a leading Jewish lawyer, about this time. An American born in 1932, Dershowitz was invited in April 2000 to a meeting in Berlin – the new German capital – where he sat on the platform and said he remembered very well how disturbed he had been to see life in Germany blossoming again so swiftly. 'No trace whatever of a troubled conscience could be perceived in any form.' Somehow he, Dershowitz, had expected that Germany's lights would stay dimmed for several years, at least in the figurative sense; instead he had had the impression that 'some time in the next five minutes [they were] all shining again at full power'.

Certainly the world had seen Willy Brandt fall to his knees in Warsaw in a grand gesture that earned him much ill-will from many conservatives. But it remained an outstanding exception. There were endless official statements of guilt from German federal governments and practically every important institution. One cannot doubt that most were sincerely meant; but we need to remind ourselves nonetheless that such protestations were a kind of required penance, performed by necessity under the eye of the distinctly international control under which Germany found itself during those years. From the outside, face was saved. Inside the country, spiting all protestations of guilt, old comrades made new careers. Just one example: a very short time after the war's end, almost the entire operational staff of Armaments Minister Albert Speer sprang revitalised to the fore to take over important levers of power. The historian Ulrich Herbert, in his prize-winning work *Specific Biographical Studies of Radicalism, Weltanschauung and Reason 1903–1989*, has described, impressively and exhaustively, the reascendance of high-ranking Nazi officials in federal Germany's postwar society.

Obviously debates took place – intellectual arguments – about Auschwitz and its everlasting consequences. Historians overwhelmed the public with their researches into the scale of the Nazi horror. There can hardly be a single village, at least in the old Federal Republic, where the story wasn't talked about and analysed – in one sense. But in another, this deeper examination of the subject seems to have remained a matter for specialists: it has not reached the broader public. It is entirely symptomatic when the writer Marcel Reich-Ranicki relates in his auto-biography *The Author of Himself* that the first person in post-Nazi Germany to ask him about his concentration-camp experiences was a journalist, in the late 1960s. Her name was Ulrike Meinhof, the future terrorist.

The Munich psychologist Louis Lewitan speaks of a conspiracy of silence in which broad swathes of the pop-ulation have participated. No one talks about it, no one asks questions. And you could certainly claim that the conspiracy has paid off. The principle of repression, of denial, of not wanting to see, has operated well: Germany has become a thriving, blossoming land, and the Germans seem – taken all in all – no more psychologically dysfunc-tional than any other people.

And perhaps it is primarily also a mixture of their own wishful thinking and conviction that makes psychologists go on researching into the long-term consequences of this neglected way of dealing with the past. Thus Tilmann

Moser has identified the 'sham cure' of this generation, a cure that will have the effect of weighing down the next generation with 'whole containerloads of problems'. His Munich colleague Wolfgang Schmidbauer is more sceptical, underlining the general jettisoning from society of the principle of 'bad conscience'. One only has to talk to the police or prosecuting lawyers, he says. 'They'll all tell you it doesn't exist any more, that a suspect never confesses or does anything positive as a result of bad conscience. All that's finished with. Now feelings of guilt only arise if you're caught.'

But Schmidbauer too reserves the right to talk about 'long-term consequences for society'. We know from countless studies, for instance, that people who repress a great deal are often anxiety-prone, awkward, resistant to all sorts of change: a state one might express as a kind of paralysis. People of this kind are poor at communicating, and their inability to resolve conflicts is frequently transferred to others. One might add to the list those who seem unwilling to allow any kind of shock or jolt into their lives – who, after the blow, might suddenly have the chance of becoming cheerful and forward-looking again. Maybe Roman Herzog[1] would have been no bad therapist after all. Is our society leaden and stifling for the additional reason that it has to chew over the past too intensively? Whatever the truth, it is amazing, Schmidbauer notes, that even the question of the extent to

---

[1] German *Bundespräsident* until 1999.

which the Third Reich has influenced life in the Federal Republic remains for many a taboo subject.

Schmidbauer talks about his relation to his own father, a soldier in the Second World War, a casualty when his son was still very young. His was a fatherless life, then, abandoned by the all-important authority figure, the central point of reference. Naturally enough, the analyst has thinned out the forest of implications for himself during long self-examination. Schmidbauer feels that the occasional states of anxiety that have accompanied him through life are connected to that early loss. He is someone who likes things to be under his control and is prone to feel anxious when something unforeseen happens. 'If I'm already in a stressed state,' he says, 'that combination of stress and powerlessness sometimes triggers the whole thing.' He offers a harmless-sounding example: he once lent his flat to a girlfriend for a few days, and then returned a day earlier than planned from an unusually strenuous business trip. His girlfriend was not at home, but as a favour for when he got back, she had been painting all the window sashes, which, as they were not yet dry, lay dismounted all over the floor. 'I stood there and felt my anxiety level rising. It was completely foolish, but something had happened that I hadn't reckoned with. In my own flat too. In my lair, if you like. Later I laughed at myself, but at the time it felt very grim.'

A tiny event, by comparison with countless greater incidents from the chasm of German history. So how are the offspring of the worst cases to succeed – and I ask the question purely theoretically – from a psychological point of view? Possibly the most important thing, according to Wolfgang Schmidbauer, would be for them to become aware that to overcome a fate like theirs is a lifelong task. They have to imagine that they are carrying a heavy weight around inside them. They need to take care that it doesn't become too heavy or too dominant. This weight, says the psychologist, must only ever be allowed to be a part of their own life, it must never be allowed to get the upper hand. Other things in life must be balanced against it: a family of one's own, work, one's own ideas, hopes. That way, maybe they won't be swallowed by the weight, says Schmidbauer. It might work like that. Something like that.

There are lighter and heavier weights; and there are the heaviest on the scales. Himmler senior would have been one of those. His only daughter would have had something very substantial to work off with him. Could she ever have managed it?

Whoever wants to write a sequel to Gudrun Himmler's story will find themselves thrown back on speculation. She has given only one interview in her life, and that was to my father. Afterwards the door was closed to the public, for ever. She made no response to my request, just as she has made no response to any of the other requests.

The book about her father – the great book of justification – has never been written, or at least it has never appeared. This does not mean, however, that she has put a distance between herself and her father. No such indications exist. Quite the contrary: a small number of facts are symptomatic of the fateful direction her life has taken.

The daughter of the late *Reichsführer-SS* continues to be involved today in a managerial capacity in an association by the name of *Stille Hilfe* – an organisation of considerable tradition. Beginning shortly after the end of the Second World War, it helped many leading National Socialists either to leave the country or to gain a fresh footing in postwar Germany. Today, according to research carried out by the *Süddeutsche Zeitung, Stille Hilfe* still boasts a good twenty members, most of them robust old Nazis. Up till 1994 it was a charitable organisation; today it is financed by donations from around a thousand sympathisers.

Old and ailing Nazis are among those helped through its discreet channels. They are nursed and cared for 'because the rest of our society has forgotten and pushed these people aside', as one member puts it. Their clientele includes, for example, Hermine Ryan, 'the mare of Majdanek'. We might imagine the SS chief's daughter and the ex-camp guard, on the latter's release, sitting down together: maybe they shared a pot of coffee and chatted about old times.

We know for certain that Frau Burwitz – as Frau Himmler became known after marrying a freelance writer of that name – regularly looks after another old person, a man residing in a home in the south of Munich. His name is Anton Malloth. Frau Burwitz regularly brings him meals and goes for walks with him. This man was *SS-Oberscharführer* at the Gestapo prison in Theresienstadt, and thus a trusted intimate of Gudrun's father. He is said to have been involved in the killing of at least seven hundred prisoners. He was known as 'the most cruel and most feared overseer in Theresienstadt', according to an extradition request issued by the Czech lawyers' association. Malloth was arrested at the end of May 2000 and is expected to have to face legal proceedings in the Czech Republic.

Frau Burwitz lives with her family in a small house in the south of Munich city. She has children of her own and is a housewife by occupation, though a housewife with a special hobby. A hobby one might as well call politics, for she cherishes not only her dear papa's fellow travellers: according to reports from a number of sources, she is also keen on appearing at meetings in the neo-Nazi calendar and happy to receive the audience's applause. As a daughter, one wonders – or also as a woman who has leadership in the blood? Has this been her way of finding an answer to the question of who she really is and what her identity amounts to, outside the shadow of her revered and overpowerful father?

The 'Nazi children' have tended to bump into each other most years. Wolf-Rüdiger Hess, Martin Bormann, Klaus von Schirach, Edda Göring: they meet at funerals or occasionally for a drink. Gudrun Burwitz, née Himmler, enjoys no great popularity. Embittered, bad-tempered, imperious and unfriendly are some of the words used to describe her. 'I don't know anyone', says one insider, 'who has ever had a good word to say about her.'

There exists a photograph of her taken in 1998 by a photographer from *Bildzeitung* on the street outside her house. A hard face, hair pulled back into a bun, boots, a string of pearls, a sportily worn scarf. The comparison may bear traces of the obvious, but she could easily pass for a leader of the *Bund der Deutschen Mädchen* in the picture. As though someone had succeeded in returning her in time, all the way back to the accursed past.

The 1959 Manuscript:

EDDA GÖRING

Hitler as Edda Göring's godfather at her christening, at
Karunhall in 1938. (Bilderdienst Süddeutscher Verlag)

A portrait of the Göring family in customary National
Socialist style in 1939. (Bilderdienst Süddeutscher Verlag)

'HAVEN'T YOU HEARD? They've closed the Reichsautobahn.'
  'How's that then?'
  'I thought everybody knew: Edda's learning to walk.'
  They used to tell that joke in Germany around 1939 or
1940. Even as a baby, Edda Göring was a star. You could
buy glossy postcards of her in every stationery store. Her
birthday – 2 June 1938 – was practically a national holiday. She came into the world in luxury, in a comfortable

bed in the Berlin West sanatorium on Joachimstalerstrasse. Hitler and the whole German Luftwaffe were her godparents.

That was twenty-two years ago. Today the baby is a young woman, slim, blonde and pretty. She lives with her mother on the fifth floor of a modern apartment block in the centre of Munich. She works in the laboratory of one of the Munich hospitals. Medical-technical assistant: that is her latest professional goal. At first she wanted to be a lawyer, but she abandoned her studies after two terms.

'Too dry for me,' she says.

Edda Göring with her mother Emmy at the time of the Nuremberg trials in 1946. (Bayerische Staatsbibliothek Bildarchiv)

'Did you ever have difficulties on account of your name?' I ask her.

'No,' she answers categorically.

And she's right. These days she finds it more of an advantage than a disadvantage to be Hermann Göring's daughter. One example would be her recent trip to Spain. She had been invited by an old friend of her father's who had set himself up in Madrid after the war and prospered. In Spain, Edda was introduced at the highest levels of society. She received invitations from the mayor of Madrid and the governor of Granada; the regime even put a car and driver at her disposal. 'Perhaps you'd like to meet Franco?' they asked.

When she was in a shop buying sunglasses and the proprietor overheard her name, he asked in broken German: 'Are you daughter . . . of real Göring?'

'Yes.'

'So, sunglass cost nothing.'

This was in 1958, in Spain.

'And Germany?' I ask.

'We have many friends here too,' says Edda Göring.

Nearly every year she goes to Bayreuth, though it is not just Richard Wagner's music that has her under its spell, but a singer too.

In the sitting room of her and her mother's flat there hangs a picture of the young Hermann Göring. Edda bears a striking similarity to her father. She has, however, a resolute lack of interest in politics. She expresses her view on the subject thus: 'If only Papi hadn't been a politician and we could all have stayed together. If only he

could have made chocolates instead, like my grandfather
did . . .'

Hermann Göring, whom Hitler had appointed his deputy,
had been sentenced to death by his own Führer in the last
days of the war. An order existed that the moment Berlin
fell, he, together with his family and entourage, was to be
shot.

Obviously the order was not carried out. Arrested at
Berchtesgaden, Göring was shipped under SS guard to
Schloss Mauterndorf, but nothing further befell him.

At Mauterndorf they were all together once more:
Göring, his wife, little Edda, her nanny, the cook, an aunt,
a niece, the chauffeur. But on 25 April they all left, travelling in several cars with their baggage train.

On the road to Zell am See, near the village of
Fischborn, the chauffeur suddenly halted. '*Herr
Reichsmarschall*, the Americans,' he announced.

The American officer spoke politely. 'I am obliged to
take you prisoner.'

Göring was brought to Zell am See. For several days
his family was allowed to remain with him. The
Reichsmarschall told his wife, 'I have a good feeling about
this.'

But his feeling deceived him. Six months later, when the
trial began in Nuremberg of the twenty-one accused of the
most serious war crimes, Göring was known as defendant number one.

In June 1945 the Americans loaded Emmy Göring, her
daughter Edda, niece, aunt, nanny and chauffeur onto a

truck and drove them from Zell am See to Veldenstein Castle in Franconia. The baggage train melted away. But despite sciatica and a sixteen-hour drive, Emmy Göring clung to her hatbox on her lap. Needless to say, the hatbox contained no hats; it contained instead all her jewellery, with an estimated value of 200,000 marks (an enormous sum in today's terms, possibly nearly half a million pounds). Until 13 October the ploy with the hatbox worked well, but on that day a CIC officer named Minskov turned up at Veldenstein, asked for Emmy Göring and announced without preamble: 'You are to hand over all your jewellery to me forthwith.'

Piece for piece, the jewels were listed by Minskov. Each time he asked: 'Who is it from?'

'From my husband,' Emmy Göring mostly answered.

At the end Minskov held up a Russian gold coin.

'Who is it from?'

'Stalin.'

'In that case you may keep it.'

Later the Görings would exchange this gold coin for a paste sausage.

On 15 October Emmy Göring was collected by the military police and taken to Straubing penitentiary.

The seven-year-old Edda moved with her nanny and the cook to a convalescent home at Neuhaus. The little girl with the long blonde ringlets was looked after by the Catholic sisters. Edda learned reading, writing and arithmetic.

On 24 November two Americans as tall as telegraph poles stepped out of an olive-green limousine and explained in English that they had to take Edda with them immediately. It was six in the evening, already dark and foggy. The two soldiers did not speak a word of German, but they were in possession of a written order.

Edda climbed into the back seat of the Americans' car with her teddy bear and a small suitcase. From time to time one of the Americans would turn and ask: 'Cold?'

'No,' Edda would reply.

At midnight they reached Straubing and Edda was thrust into her mother's cell.

'Actually I found it very comfortable there,' Edda Göring remembers. She slept on a chequered blanket that had once been sent as a gift by Mussolini to Karinhall, and which had a high souvenir value among the occupying soldiers at Straubing. On 6 December Edda was even visited by St Nicholas. One of the prisoners dressed up and knocked at the cell door. Edda recited a poem and in return was given a gift of little men made of bread.

In Nuremberg, at about the same time, the American deputy prosecutor Ralph G. Albrecht addressed the International Military Tribunal in the following terms: 'We now turn to the facts in the case of perhaps the most important conspirator sitting in this courtroom, to the Nazi number two Hermann Göring. To a Nazi who stood alongside the Führer, to the Nazi who in many regards was more dangerous than the Führer and other leading men of the Party. We maintain that he was perhaps more dangerous, because he came from a good family. He possessed good looks, charm and a certain affability. But all these qualities were deceptive . . .'

'Had you managed to have any contact with your husband by this time?' I ask Emmy Göring.

'Yes. I received a letter from him in an unexpectedly dramatic way. The prisoner who distributed our meals passed it to me in our cell.'

'So the letter was smuggled all the way from the prison at Nuremberg to the Straubing penitentiary?'

'Yes.'

After they had been at Straubing for four months, the camp commandant came into the Görings' cell one morning. It was 19 February 1946. 'Yesterday evening I received the order to set you and your daughter at liberty.'

'At liberty – where?' asked Emmy Göring.

'I don't know.'

The wife of the once so powerful *Reichsmarschall*, the mistress of Karinhall, did not know either, and found herself asking the commandant for a few days' grace. He agreed to postpone their release for a few days. But twelve days later he was standing in their cell again. 'I can give you another week, then you'll have to disappear.'

During that last week an American journalist named Peggy Poor arrived at Straubing with the intention of getting an exclusive interview with Emmy Göring for her newspaper.

'I don't give interviews,' was the response of the wife of defendant number one – 'unless you could find us a flat.'

Peggy Poor could and did. She got her interview, and in March 1946 Emmy and Edda Göring moved to a small hunting lodge in the Fränkischer Wald near Sackdilling, where they were tenants of a forester family named Frank.

The nearest village was an hour and a half away. The public health officer gave little Edda a certificate excusing her from the long journey to and from school on grounds of her delicate health, and Emmy Göring taught her daughter at home.

'I had to learn an awful lot of poetry,' Edda remembers of her mother's tuition. 'Poetry, songs and naturally my two-times table.'

The Nuremberg trial, which had already lasted almost a year, was entering its final phase. After a first step, when the censorship of mail between the principal defendants and their families had been eased, the court now authorised the families to visit.

The Görings stayed in Nuremberg from 14 to 29 September, at the home of the attorney Dr Stahmer, Hermann Göring's defence counsel. There was half an hour's visiting time approved for every day of the week except Sundays. On the seventh day Edda was allowed to accompany her mother for the first time.

'You mustn't cry, whatever you do,' Emmy impressed on her daughter.

Edda managed not to cry. She waved to her father through the pane of glass and told him happily: 'It's so nice that I'm allowed to see you.' During his imprisonment Göring had lost twenty-seven kilos in weight. Suddenly seeing his daughter before him, he lost his composure for a moment and wept. The security guards in their white helmets stood like statues behind him.

'You've grown,' said Hermann Göring.

'And I know lots of poems. Shall I tell you one?'

'Yes.'

'"*I dream I am a child once more,*"' Edda recited solemnly, '"*and I shake my greying head . . .*"'

On 29 September all families were required to leave Nuremberg again. The next day Hermann Göring, as the first of the accused, heard his sentence: 'Death by hanging.' German radio broadcast the words to the hunting lodge near Sackdilling.

Emmy Göring had sent Edda out for a walk, but it was clear the news couldn't be hidden from her daughter. If Edda didn't hear it from her mother, she would certainly hear it from strangers. Emmy merely added: 'The sentence probably won't be carried out. Papi will probably be exiled to an island somewhere.'

Of the twenty-one principal defendants at Nuremberg, eleven were sentenced to death. Ten walked to the gallows in the night of 16 October 1946, but in Göring's case the sentence was indeed not carried out. He had obtained a capsule of poison and the previous day had taken his own life.

Edda remained at Sackdilling until 1948. She was now ten and had never spent a day at school. Emmy Göring continued to teach her according to her own precise timetable.

In July 1948 the Görings moved out of the hunting lodge to a rundown house on the outskirts of Etzelwang in the Oberpfalz.

Emmy Göring had herself announced to the headmistress of the secondary school in Sulzbach-Rosenberg. 'I would be very grateful if you would take Edda into your school.'

'Do you have her reports?' asked the headmistress.

'Edda doesn't have any reports.'

'Then I'm afraid not.'

'Couldn't she take the entrance examination without reports?'

Edda was finally allowed to sit the exam. She passed with flying colours. As a final test – a trick question – she was asked to recite the Lord's Prayer and the Ten Commandments. When she recited both without error, the headmistress said: 'There's nothing else for it, I really am going to have to take you on.'

In lieu of her first report, she was awarded a book prize. The headmistress explained the reason: 'If we had given her a report, we would have had to give her such good marks that the other parents might have complained that we were favouring Göring's girl.'

In 1951 Emmy Göring found a flat in the Tengstrasse in Munich. She called on the headmaster of St Anna's secondary school to ask for her daughter to be enrolled.

'What is your name, please?'

'Emmy Göring.'

The headmaster looked up in astonishment. 'What are the other children going to say?'

'Nothing, I would imagine. They didn't say anything at Sulzbach-Rosenberg.'

So Edda entered the second year of St Anna's secondary school for girls and stayed there till her *Abitur*.

'From her first day Edda was a model schoolgirl,' one

of her classmates told me. 'She was never late. She never forgot her books or her homework. Ticking-off and detention – they were unknown words to Edda.'

Only once, in the seventh year, in Latin, did she get a four.

Whenever the girls read classical plays – Schiller's *Maria Stuart* or Hebbel's *Agnes Bernauer* – Edda always took the leading role. The name of Hermann Göring barely cropped up during history lessons. The teacher took the girls as far as the First World War. About the Third Reich she merely commented: 'We don't have any time to follow that up just now. I suggest you take your books and read about it at home.'

'Do you think', I ask the former St Anna's pupil, 'she said that out of consideration for Edda Göring?'

'I'm sure she did.'

The girl with the corkscrew ringlets was shown great consideration, and not just in history classes. 'At school we never talked about the past,' said Edda. 'And politics was completely taboo anyway.'

In the girls' dancing lessons Edda was again favoured, the dancing teacher frequently choosing her for solo spots. A local company gave her a motorcycle as a present. Gründgens invited her to the theatre in Düsseldorf.[1]

In 1958 she passed her *Abitur*. With flying colours, naturally. Her essay subject was a phrase of Theodor Heuss's: 'To forget is simultaneously a kindness and a peril.'

---

[1] Gustav Gründgens was a famous actor and director, and a leading theatrical personality under the Nazis.

'You will travel a hard road,' Hans Frank had written to his son Norman, 'for you bear my name . . .'

For Edda Göring, the gloomy prognosis of one of those hanged at Nuremberg has not applied. She has never really stopped being the golden girl she was when she was born.

'Farah Diba received sixteen thousand telegrams for her crown prince,' says Emmy Göring. 'When Edda was born, there were six hundred and twenty-eight thousand!'

Edda on her way to school in Munich. (Hulton Getty)

A Sightseeing Tour of Munich
in the Year 2000

THIS TOO WAS taboo for a long time. What kind of fate is it to be a National Socialist's son or daughter, the child of one of the evildoers, of a murderer? How do you deal with it? How much do you suffer from it? To ask the question another way: Is a leading Nazi's son or daughter a victim too? One might argue that a Nazi's offspring find themselves somewhere on the boundary between perpetrators and victims, insofar as they are forced to take a position on what their father did. We must ask ourselves: Are they, do they become, do they think, exactly like their fathers? And as for victimhood, aren't they haunted their whole life through by a curse arising from events for which, in truth, they bear no responsibility?

In Germany the subject was simply avoided for a long time. People seemed to feel that to tackle it would instantly and dangerously transform past into future. But even in other countries, these questions were frequently faced in a less than open-minded way. When the psychologist Dan Bar-On in the 1980s published his conversations with descendants of Nazis, he found himself on the receiving end of extreme hostility. The criticism ran: How, as a Jew, could he allow himself to get so close to the perpetrators, and in such an emotional fashion? With the possible consequence that he might end up with feelings of compassion for their children? How could Germans be turned into victims?

When my father's series first appeared in *Weltbild*, it attracted dozens of readers' letters that were also published. Some were accusatory in tone: Why do you tell the stories of these Nazi families with such emotion when you could be devoting yourself to the fate of their victims? One Erich Bragenheim from Verden an der Aller wrote:

> . . . is it absolutely essential for you to set before your readers a picture of how these children of Germany's former gravediggers live today? By doing so you are merely uselessly, and violently, reopening old wounds for the victims of these children's parents. By and large you show that once again these children are living in decent circumstances, and that some of them at least have remained loyal to the old ideologies, while the victims' children for the most part still live lives of impoverishment and have been unable to reach key positions in their professions.

But there were also numerous letters in a different tenor. Barbara Fischer from Bonn, for instance, wrote:

I have been reading your series of reports with great interest . . . I think with the greatest regret of the Goebbels daughters, who were killed by their own parents' hands. They might still be living today, like Edda Göring, the Frank boys or the 'batty' Himmler girl . . .

And a Frau Otto from Bonn wrote:

I read that Dr Jürgen Fijalkowski wishes to cancel his subscription to your magazine because you have brought to your readers' attention the stories of the Nazi bosses' children, boys and girls who are now getting on with respectable lives and who, at the time when their fathers ruled Germany, had no idea of what their fathers were really doing. If your readers really wish to be scandalised, they need look no further than the shameless behaviour of 'BB'.

A recent edition of the magazine had carried a lengthy report about the life of the young Brigitte Bardot.

The series entitled 'For You Bear My Name' ended in 1960. The article that told Edda Göring's story finished on a remarkable note. The name Göring had been terrifically useful to her, she said, it had been an excellent name to have in Germany. She said this with fifteen years' experience of life in postwar Germany, fourteen years after her father's death by his own hand a few hours before he was due to hang. She gave her grounds for her conviction.

She thought that the Germans had quite simply been fond of her father; and then there had been his many excellent contacts abroad, which she had found she could still make use of decades later. And sometimes, well, there were those little creature comforts that just made life pleasant, like the complimentary tickets for premieres at the Bayreuth Festival; the Wagner family had not forgotten her. (A postscript to Bayreuth: when Wolf-Rüdiger Hess heard that Edda routinely received gifts of comps for the festival, he – the son of Hitler's deputy – asked the Wagner household whether he might not also be included on the list. Of course, came the reply. Since when he too has received free tickets in the post.)

Of course it remains questionable whether it has truly been advantageous to be called Edda Göring. A conspicuous factor in the argument is that the Nazi children who have never disavowed their fathers – Wolf-Rüdiger Hess, Gudrun Himmler – are the ones who have consistently declared, right up to the year 2000, that they have only ever benefited from their father's legacy. There seems to be a connection there: a child that so passionately deifies its father draws from his pretended significance and one-time lustre a considerable part of its own sense of itself – and is simultaneously incapable of owning up that its family history is, in truth, a serious psychological handicap. Given such a self-created version of the truth, how can one admit to the existence of a family flaw? Thus do men and women sometimes furnish their world, with windows so narrow that they look out each day only on what is acceptable to the frightened seeing eye.

Thus, in a sense, has Edda Göring also organised her life. She still lives in Munich, in the small flat in the Lehel district that she shared with Emmy until her mother's death. The walls of the flat are hung with many photos and paintings of her father and mother. People who have visited the apartment mention how much it looks like a Göring museum. Today Edda is sixty-two years old, still single, never married. Among those who know her there is talk of one possible relationship: she is thought to have been close to a journalist who was passionately interested in her father's life story. In other words, someone who would not drag her father's name through the mud, who would, like her, honour and respect him.

I'm not sure I would have questioned Edda about the finer points of her private life. Maybe I would have; the details are often salutary. How, for example, does a relationship, a close friendship, work when – to put it with a certain bluntness – there's a big fat corpse down in the basement? Other people will fall in love with a person who has the same inclinations as they do, the same tastes, someone who enjoys books and the theatre, or sport, whatever means a lot to them. If you were Frau Göring, wouldn't you in that case fall in love with someone who felt the same as you did, at least by extension, so to speak, someone for whom the most important thing in your life – your father – was something they treasured equally?

Edda's views on the matters of fundamental importance in her life have been clearly stated. In an interview with *Quick* magazine in 1986 she said: 'I still feel bound to my parents by a great love. I have my parents' love and kindness to thank for my wonderful childhood. I feel very moved when I think of the way my father took care of me. I have good memories of him.' Of the days, for example, when 'my dear godfather' Adolf Hitler came to visit, Edda reported: 'From the circumstances, from everything that went on around me, I realised even as a little girl that he must be something special. He brought me liquorice sweets which he knew I loved and which he made sure he always had with him, specially for me.' Of her overweight father's eccentric lifestyle and his flamboyant dress sense, she said: 'My father was a great one for the baroque period. Perhaps he developed a habit of dressing that was a little bit ahead of his time – especially when you think how much care young people take these days to dress up in that fantastic way of theirs.'

To the American journalist Gerald Posner she explained ten years later: 'Now you know how I feel. I love him very much, and people really shouldn't expect me to judge him in any other way. He was a good father to me, and I have always missed him. That's all I will say to you.'

In everything spoken and written about Edda Göring, one thing is perfectly clear: she is much too clever to call into question the crimes committed in the name of National Socialism. She has spoken repeatedly of the dreadful years and of the 'unspeakable misery many had to suffer under the Hitler regime'. Yet she never seems to have felt a personal sense of horror for all the suffering wrought in the name of Göring and company. Thus she continues to feel that a great wrong was done to her family when its assets were confiscated after the war's end. And they were substantial, since Göring, in true robber-knight fashion, had amassed a colossal fortune, mainly in the form of art treasures. Edda's papa had, for example, instructed the city of Cologne to present its *Madonna and Child* by Lucas Cranach to his daughter on the occasion of her birth in 1938. In a decade-long lawsuit Edda bitterly fought Cologne for the return of 'her' Cranach (approximate value: 100,000 marks). She lost the case. The grounds were illuminating: Papa Göring had not lawfully acquired the painting.

In his book *Burdened*, Gerald Posner compared Edda Göring to Wolf-Rüdiger Hess in two respects: her furious anger towards the Nuremberg tribunal and her deep loathing for all ideas and values belonging to the United States. Like Hess, she criticises Germany for allowing itself to be influenced far too easily by the United States. And for being far too little opposed to all the evils – drugs, prostitution, mass poverty – that wash over Germany from there. You could formulate their feelings slightly differently: Germany doesn't generate nearly enough German politics for Edda's and Wolf-Rüdiger's liking. To which you would presumably have their agreement if you were to add: the kind their fathers made.

Hess, Schirach, Bormann, Göring, Himmler. And looming over all these and the others, always and for ever, the figure of Adolf Hitler. They constituted the core of German National Socialism, sometimes fond of each other, sometimes not; they courted Hitler, striving for recognition and power, occasionally fighting each other openly. The mesh of these relations plays a role still in the lives of their children. My daddy's enemy is my enemy. In addition, practically every one of their offspring, Martin Bormann and Niklas Frank excepted, has framed for him- or herself their own historical image of the father, something along the lines of: he was all right, maybe a little too loyal to the Führer as things turned out, but it was the others who were the real villains. Edda Göring was once quoted as saying that obviously it was incomparably harder to be a daughter of Heinrich Himmler than a daughter of Hermann Göring – adding, as the others might equally have claimed for their fathers, that hers had never been an anti-Semite, that was an incontrovertible fact. To this or that Jew, for instance, he had been the soul of kindness . . .

Edda Göring refused my invitation to be interviewed. She informed me that she well remembered the conversation she had had with my father forty years ago, and that she had kept his article. But for another long interview she was at this time unavailable. She would prefer people to leave her in peace and to attend to those who had had to live through the DDR dictatorship instead, which was a far more pressing question and far more interesting.

I can't say I was particularly sad that our meeting didn't happen. An enormous weariness overcame me at the thought of sitting opposite yet another person who had armoured the door to their life to such an extent that one no longer cared to knock at it. This is a hazard of visiting the Nazi children: those who lead a petrified existence and the others who have let doubt and rage, powerlessness and truth, into their lives, and begun something one might call a high-wire walk, a walk without a safety net over a deep abyss. And no one knows when, or how, it will end.

The city of Munich offers great opportunities for a sightseeing tour into the past. In the attractive Lehel district in the middle of the city lives Frau Göring, not very far from Herr von Schirach. Over to the west, in one of the suburbs, lives Herr Hess. In another suburb, at Neuried, you will find Frau Burwitz, née Himmler. There is probably no special reason for this; Munich was once the movement's capital, and when a tribe has made camp somewhere it can stay for a long time. This is as true of Munich as of anywhere else. But perhaps it is also partly due to the climate of this friendly, peaceful city, where one can live out one's life so wonderfully undisturbed. And maybe it doesn't hurt either to be able to seek out from time to time the odd location redolent with history.

About twenty kilometres from Munich lies the village of Ebenhausen. Lots of green, an *S-Bahn* station, a big supermarket, a nursing home for the elderly, pretty family homes. People like the life here, with the big city nearby. This is where Karl-Otto Saur lives with his family; the attractive villa with a garden also holds the offices of his media company. Here in his office we talked over the space of two afternoons. On both days it was already dark by the time I drove home again.

Karl-Otto Saur junior told me that he had been tempted once or twice to write about himself and his father: how did it feel as an enlightened left-winger to have had a high-ranking Nazi in the family? In 1987, writing for the *Süddeutsche Zeitung*, he had watched every episode of the American television series *Holocaust* when it was pre-viewed to selected German journalists. On another occasion he had sat on a jury judging television films and documentary entries on the subject of the Third Reich. Saur remembers how much these experiences disturbed him at the time. Each time in the train on his way back to Munich he had started to write something about his family history. 'Now I'll do it, I thought.' And he wrote about the television series, about particular aspects of the film festival, but nothing about himself and his father. He says he doesn't know exactly why he has never managed to do it. He says he is certain that his anxiety that 'an arti-cle like that could come across as vain' played a part. 'I didn't want that.'

Vanity? Perhaps it is a reason. Perhaps he also had a feeling that made him shrink from putting the story on public display, maybe a voice warned him not to get too close to the subject for as long as he wasn't absolutely sure he would be able to cope with it.

Karl-Otto tells the story of the little cigar box. The Saur family had to scrape to get by after the Second World War. They were extremely poor; their diet was dominated by semolina and barley broth, and an ice-cream cone for ten pfennigs from the baker's was the greatest treat. New clothes were out of the question, and the younger children were permanently dressed in hand-me-downs. Even today, Karl-Otto says, this remains a problem for him: the family eats up what's on their plates – and naturally nothing ever gets thrown away just because the sell-by date has expired. He has to grin as he says it. You can imagine, he says, how this basic outlook of mine leads to constant difficulties in my relations with my children and grand-children. 'Naturally I do try to mend my ways, but you can't really ask much more than that from an old man.'

It was at the beginning of the 1950s that Karl-Otto, born in 1944 and about six or seven years old at the time, one day found the cigar box in a cupboard. Medals lay inside, medals of iron with his father's name on them. And photos in which his father was in uniform, often in the centre of the snapshot, surrounded by others looking up at him. In several of them there was a man with a moustache – Adolf Hitler. 'I remembered the feeling I felt the first time I laid eyes on those things. It was a lot like pride. My father had been important. There had been times when we hadn't been poor.' Saur says that until then he had thought of his father in quite a different way: as a man who never earned enough money, a man no one looked up to, a loser. 'I can still remember feeling a bit more important myself when I found those old things.'

As he says, he remembered the feeling well; perhaps it burned itself into his memory. For in later life he is shocked by it. And this is also a potential danger: you get involved with your father, you hate him, you condemn him, possibly in public – and your life has a bit more meaning because of it. So your own identity is still partly determined, so to speak, by the fact that your father spent a fair amount of his time in the vicinity of Adolf Hitler.

Karl-Otto Saur had basically experienced the feeling Wolfgang Schmidbauer has warned of: anybody with a family history of that kind had better take care that their father doesn't move into pole position in their own soul.

Karl-Otto's father, Karl-Otto Saur senior, was what we would call today a manager: a fixer. He had come to the firm of Thyssen in the 1920s after his family's business in Freiburg went broke during the postwar slump. At Thyssen's he had risen rapidly. And had been immediately smitten by the new party, the NSDAP. He joined in 1931 and from the outset mixed freely with other members of the National Socialist Guild of German Engineers, finally moving to Munich in order to work as a kind of right hand to the future minister for armaments Fritz Todt. When Todt lost his life in a mysterious air crash and the Plenipotentiary for Building Albert Speer took over as his successor, Saur was given the role of deputy. His bosses waxed enthusiastic about him: perfect work every time, they said. He was praised by all for his organisational talent, as a master at putting plans into effect. Hitler, in his 'political testament', named Saur as Speer's successor as Reich minister for armaments and war production. Only those who occupied levels beneath Saur in the hierarchy were less enthusiastic. To them he was an ill-tempered and brutal man consumed by a lust for power.

He thought of everything, provided for every eventuality. For the stepping-up of wartime production, for the resupply of forced labourers, whose work for the Reich was often synonymous with death. Thus Karl-Otto Saur was one of those whose efforts brought about so much horror that six decades later it is still around. The present discussion about the final level of damages to be paid by the German federal government and German industry has a great deal to do with the activities of Karl-Otto Saur.

For his son, it is entirely clear that the father, taking over every task, basically organised everything. Everything, even the camps. It was more by chance than anything else that his father's deeds were no worse. The extent of his collaboration in the deeds of others is nevertheless immense. 'He undoubtedly has a hell of a lot of blood on his hands,' says my former colleague. In the early 1990s, when the records were opened, Saur junior travelled to Berlin to look at the rules and orders that regulated the flow of forced labourers towards the end of the war. And at the bottom of several such papers, 'there was my father's signature', he says. 'Of course I knew his signature. There was nothing surprising for me about being confronted with my father's responsibility, but at that moment, seeing his handwriting, I felt someone had stuck a knife into me.'

His father was taken into custody by the Americans in 1945. This time they were not interested in an indictment: they had other plans for the insider from the heart of the National Socialists' engine room. They made him an offer: Tell us what you know, turn state's evidence in the trial against the big guys at Krupp – and we'll leave you alone. This was because the Americans wanted a show trial that would demonstrate the collective guilt of German industry. Saur accepted, and with his testimony helped to bring about Krupp's conviction.

In 1948 the Americans released Karl-Otto senior. By German industry he was viewed as the great traitor, and the word went out. His old colleagues at Speer's ministry almost all had great careers ahead of them: Dorsch and Hettlage, Mommsen, Schlieker and the rest. That would make a story too, Karl-Otto had thought on his journey home: the success stories of his father's old fellow combatants. It would have plenty to say about postwar Germany. But not that easy for a son to write. It could be mistaken for a son's complaint against his father for being a failure in life.

The elder Saur remained unsuccessful until his death in 1966. An engineering consultancy, a small publishing house; nothing came to anything. The publishing house enjoyed its first success when the elder son, Klaus, took over the business. Today the K. G. Saur Verlag is a well-known name. From its presses in recent years there have come several academic studies relating to the Holocaust and the crimes of the National Socialists – unprofitable works from any economic standpoint. 'For me,' Klaus says, 'it's a kind of reparation, if you like.'

Within the family, the Saurs never spoke about the past. The children asked no questions of their father. 'We couldn't have anyhow, knowing what my father was like. It was out of the question,' says Karl-Otto. Nor of his mother. 'From her we only got kind of empty husks of words – "Where there's light, there are always shadows" and such nonsense.' There was silence to the grave. 'For me my father was a father, first and foremost, and a pretty bad one,' he says. And cowardly to boot: for years he carried on a secret relationship with his secretary, a woman who had stayed with him throughout and till his death never strayed from his side. His marriage was a sham he acted out for years, with Karl-Otto's mother and everyone else.

During our conversations we reached a point from time to time where I had the feeling that it had become very quiet in the room and that nothing existed outside its four walls. It seemed to happen each time Karl-Otto talked about the part of his father he felt within himself. The mainspring of his father's motivation, he said, was boundless opportunism. 'And I feel the same in me. There have been situations in my professional life when I've felt that opportunism in me to the point that I've done exactly the opposite of what it told me to do, simply because I didn't want to be like him.'

Karl-Otto doesn't make things easy for himself. He talks about having sometimes asked himself how he would have behaved in his father's place back then, during the dictatorship. And he finds no answer. He talks about not knowing what he would have done if the Americans had punished his father more severely and sentenced him, like Speer, to a long custodial sentence. Would he have broken with him, disowned him? 'Probably not,' he says, and adds: 'Though I didn't love my father, at least I believe I would have stood by him. I had the feeling early on that I was completely alone in the world. When he died, I didn't cry.'

In the editorial offices he has worked in, he says, he has frequently asked himself what would have become of his colleagues back then. Who would have been a Nazi? Who a perpetrator, who a fellow traveller? He can't get this thought out of his head. Maybe it's also the reason, he says, why success and career were never concepts that were important to him in the sense of 'a life that works out'. In what is an astonishingly sentimental admission for him, he says he has had only one aim in life: to be a better father to his children than his own father was. 'I wanted to achieve a loving, open relationship with them, critical too, but it was really only about one thing: I wanted them to know that whatever happens, it doesn't matter, I'm there for them.'

Has the subject of his father become more important over the years or less? It's astonishing, he says, 'but it gets more and more important. The older I get, the more I find it preoccupying me.' Which is why, he says, it's a nonsense to demand that people now put an end to all this examination of the past. 'The opposite is true. Slowly it's all receding far enough for us to be able to tell the right stories about it at last.'

As I said, each day it was dark by the time I drove home. Today when I think back to these conversations with Karl-Otto, I see an image before me: a man surrounded by the pans of scales to whose contents he has for years and years been carefully adding and subtracting, in order not to lose his balance.

The 1959 Manuscript:

THE VON SCHIRACH BROTHERS

THE YOUNG MAN studies the shop window for a couple of minutes. Then he steps hesitantly into the elegant chemist's shop.

'Can I help you?' asks a blonde woman in a light-blue silk shop coat.

'I want some soap,' the young man answers.

'For a lady?'

'No, for a man – something special, please.'

The blonde woman spreads a wide selection on the counter for him. German, English, French soaps. Some he immediately puts to one side. These are the ones he has bought in past years, and he has decided he will buy a different soap each year. He finally selects an English soap, light brown in colour and packed in a small but luxurious sandalwood box.

The young man walks slowly up the Kurfürstendamm. He walks against the stream of passers-by. Most people have left their coats at home today. It is spring in Berlin.

The sky is pale blue, the sun is shining, and the lilac is in bloom.

Only the world of politics looks black once again. The Paris four-power conference has broken down even before it started. The Soviet leader Khrushchev has been issuing ominous threats. The morning papers in Berlin have appeared with disturbing banner headlines.

The city is nervous.

They'll probably confiscate the sandalwood box, thinks the young man. Sandalwood must be forbidden.

Only two items are allowed as presents: soap and pipes. Both his brothers always take pipes. He and his sister are responsible for soap. Variety is important.

As he does every time, he feels uneasy as he turns into the Wilhelmstrasse in Spandau. He stands hesitantly in front of the great redbrick building with its battlements and towers. The grey door is locked. The windows are barred. Behind the metre-thick walls crowned with broken glass runs an iron fence, and between the two a high-voltage installation. The watchtowers are manned day and night.

For fourteen years the fortress at Spandau has been under four-power Allied command. The very system that broke down in Paris works here: Russians, Americans, British and French all sing from the same hymn sheet. Each country has in place a prison governor and a guard detachment. In addition there are two cooks, a hairdresser, twenty prison warders and twenty-seven further officials.

Of the thirty-three prison cells at Spandau, thirty stand

empty. The whole mighty apparatus is maintained for three prisoners; according to prison regulations they have no names, only numbers. Number one is Hitler's Reich youth leader Baldur von Schirach, number five is Hitler's minister for armaments Albert Speer, number seven is Hilter's deputy Rudolf Hess.

Each prisoner has a cell measuring three by four metres. Each is led daily into the courtyard and allowed 1,500 steps. Each is allowed once a week to write a letter of 1,300 words. And each is allowed once a month to receive a visit.

The bells in the tower of the Melanchthonkirche strike nine o'clock. The young man crosses the Wilhelmstrasse to the redbrick building. A couple of passers-by turn and watch him with interest.

'My name is Robert von Schirach,' says the young man to the guard at the gate, taking a written permit from his briefcase. 'I'd like to speak to my father.'

As always, there now begins a long procedure, at the end of which Robert von Schirach puts his signature to a protocol in which he undertakes not to shake his father's hand, make any gestures or speak about politics, and to keep to the authorised visiting time of half an hour.

While Robert is signing, an Allied guard is unlocking Schirach's cell. 'Number one, follow me. Visiting day.'

When Robert is led into the Spandau visitors' room, his father is already sitting on a chair. A broad table is the barrier between the two. A soldier walks up and down in the room. Depending on the timetable, it is an American, a Briton, a Frenchman or a Russian. He counts the minutes.

When the thirty minutes are up, he separates the white-haired prisoner from his son.

'Till the next time, Paps.'

'Till the next time, Robs.'

The next time will fall due six months from now.

Robert von Schirach is twenty-two. He works in a printing shop in Trossingen. His boss is a former adjutant of his father's. He is what people call a successful young man. He drives a company car, earns a good salary, and spends most of his free time sitting on a horse. He rides in events and dreams of becoming a farmer in Africa.

He has a sister and two brothers. Angelika lives in Hamburg as a painter. The elder brother, Richard, is a junior lawyer in Munich. Klaus, the younger, is still at school. They share the twelve Spandau visits out among themselves. Schirach's letters are always addressed to Angelika. Each of the children has a paragraph devoted to them. Angelika cuts the letters into strips and forwards them.

'Dear Robert,' Schirach wrote in a recent letter,

your report on your ankle doesn't reassure me at all. You are to go and get it – the ankle – X-rayed immediately, do you hear? If you don't go to the doctor at once, I shall never write you another word. You have no idea what kind of complications can arise simply from your ignoring your ankle. The 'loving care' of your dancing partner, an energetic doctor, and a few weeks in plaster is better for you . . .

'What do you talk about with your father when you sit opposite him for half an hour in Spandau?' I ask.

'Because he takes as much interest as he can – in the circumstances – in our interests, the contact is there already,' Robert answers. 'He and I talk a great deal about horses. With my brother Richard he talks about Richard's trumpet-playing. And with Angelika, obviously they talk about art.'

'How does he manage to keep up with all those things in prison?'

'The prisoners are allowed books in unlimited quantities. My father reads a great deal.'

'About trumpet-playing . . .?'

'Apparently.'

'Visitors to the war criminals' jail at Spandau have to submit to a wide range of security measures. Can you give me some idea of what they are?'

'I can't tell you anything about that,' the young Schirach replies. 'We have to undertake not to give out any information about internal matters.'

'What will happen if you do?'

'I'd have my permit to visit revoked.'

Up to now Spandau's rule of secrecy has functioned perfectly. From the fastness of the prison, scant news makes it into the outside world. The news received by the inmates is carefully censored. The prisoners receive two newspapers, though only in garbled form. Articles, mainly about politics, are simply cut out.

Rudolf Hess was sentenced to life imprisonment, but for Speer and Schirach the doors of Spandau will open in

The von Schirach brothers: from left to right, Robert, Klaus and Richard. (Bilderdienst Süddeutscher Verlag)

six years' time. They will have served twenty years to the day. From that moment on, the Reich youth leader who once composed for the Hitler Youth a song entitled 'Our Banner Flutters Out Before Us' will be able to contemplate a carefree future. He is the heir to a substantial fortune left him by an American aunt. The former youth leader was born to a titled father and an American mother. The stock portfolio he inherited in 1952, securely invested in US railroad stocks, originally belonged to his grandmother Elizabeth Bolly Norris of Philadelphia.

When Baldur von Schirach is released in 1966, he will be sixty. When the thousand-year Reich imploded, he was not quite forty. He remained at his residence as governor of Vienna until the end. His wife and four children went into hiding in the Tyrol mountains.

It is 4 May 1945.

Henriette von Schirach stands on the terrace of a mountain hotel and looks down at Kufstein. The American armoured spearhead is advancing into the town from the direction of Kiefersfelden. People are pouring into the streets, waving handkerchiefs and bunches of flowers.

The fire has gone out, as the Tyrolean farmers say.

The Reich youth leader's wife has two items in her possession: her husband's last letter and, packed in light-blue cotton wool, several capsules of poison. The letter begins with the phrase 'As I write, the guns are thundering outside Vienna' and ends with the Latin expression '*Fortuna fortes adiuvat*' (Fortune favours the brave). Of practical advice there is none. (The poison capsules are distributed by an office in the Reich Chancellery.)

The Schirachs, here in Hintertux bei Kufstein, will not poison themselves. Henriette's view is that life goes on. Seven-year-old Robert is up in the pasture with the cows – he's happy where he is and he could hardly be asked to understand the reasons for taking potassium cyanide.

On 9 May the first American soldiers arrive in Hintertux, cheerful boys who drink red wine and hand out chewing gum to the children. They have no idea whose children these are in front of them . . .

Next day, less friendly Americans arrive. They ransack the small hotel from top to bottom, even stripping Henriette of her wedding ring. Curiously they vanish with everyone's identity papers. For the Schirachs this is no loss, quite the opposite: this way they lose a name that no longer possesses any value anyway.

The wildest rumours reach Hintertux about Baldur von Schirach. He has been hanged from the Florisdorf bridge in Vienna; he has fled to Switzerland. He has gone over to the Russians with Rendulic. The truth is eventually revealed on the radio: 'Schirach has given himself up to the Americans.'

The Americans in the Tyrol meanwhile are settling in and making themselves comfortable. The first Rainbow Clubs are opening. The soldiers are singing new, non-German songs in their barrack squares. 'You are my sunshine, my only sunshine . . .'

On 21 June a large car drives into Hintertux. A captain named Hansen gets out. '*Snell maken,*' he tells Henriette in broken German. 'I'm taking you to Baldur.'

Hansen is entirely serious. In a prison camp outside Innsbruck Henriette von Schirach is able to talk to her husband for half an hour.

'Why are you doing this for us?' she asks on the return journey.

'We're related,' Captain Hansen replies. 'My mother was a Middleton and Baldur's mother was a Middleton too, from the South. We found out during his questioning.'

Eventually the Schirachs make their way back to Bavaria on a refugee train. Thanks to their stolen papers, the family travels by the name of Sandham. From Munich they drive in a van to Kochel, where the Reich youth leader and his family once lived in the small castle of Aspenstein. In the meantime it has been turned into an American headquarters, and the Schirachs are forced to live in one of the adjacent buildings. In the evenings Robert is sent to spy on the Americans and to find out how things look in the 'big house'.

'It all seemed very cheerful,' the young Schirach remembers today. 'They were always celebrating birthdays. One of the officers put on my father's Reich leader uniform for fun.'

Robert made friends with a Polish boy who had been freed by the Americans from a concentration camp and taken along with them. His parents had both been murdered in the camp. The residents of Kochel shook their heads, but the friendship endured. Here, where everyone knew the Schirachs, they could no longer go by their false name. Once a week CIC officers arrived and interrogated the wife of the Reich youth leader.

'How often did you go to Auschwitz?'

'I've never been.'

'You're lying,' said the officer. He went on: 'Have you ever shot anyone yourself?'

'No.'

'Where have you hidden the stolen jewels of the Empress Maria Theresa?'

Always the same questions repeated. Were you Hitler's

lover? Where is Eva Braun? Is it true Baldur's an adopted child and is really called Meyer? Is it true that he is homosexual?

In the following months the Schirachs moved several times. From Kochel to a hunting lodge in Urfeld. Then to a country hotel in the Jachenau. Henriette was arrested three times and three times released again, for the final time in 1948.

Before then she travelled – as did most of the other leading Nazi wives – several times to Nuremberg to visit her husband. She was even interrogated on that account when she returned home again.

'Are you often in Nuremberg?'

'Yes.'

'Do you go to parties there?'

'No.'

'But you're having an affair with a prosecutor named Thomas Dodd.'

'I don't know any Mr Dodd.'

'Do you swear it?'

Henriette von Schirach swore that she had not had and was not having an affair with the Nuremberg prosecutor Thomas Dodd. She was made to swear on the Bible, her hand on the embossed gold of the cross.

Today in Baldur von Schirach's cell in Spandau there also hangs a cross. It was carved for him at Oberammergau. On his small table stand the pictures of his three sons and his daughter. His wife's picture is missing.

Henriette von Schirach divorced her husband in 1950 and took her maiden name of Hoffmann again.

Why?

When, after her divorce before the Munich *Landgericht*, it was announced in the press that she had dissolved her marriage because she could not be expected to remain the wife of a war criminal, Henriette brought a private action against an editor in Hamburg and defended herself in an open letter to the *Süddeutsche Zeitung*:

'I have never at any time used that language. It has been made manifest by me, in four tribunal hearings and seventeen interrogations, that Baldur von Schirach is no war criminal, he is an idealist, and much too good for politics . . .'

Frau von Schirach probably meant by this that during much of his lifetime Baldur had composed poetry. Once he used to sing:

'How wounded are our fervent hearts, how
    faded our banners flying,
Around each mother's tired mouth there plays a
    strange foreboding . . .'

He still composes poetry. When in 1948 he succeeded in smuggling a message out to his wife, he wrote this on the scrap of paper: 'We didn't recognise the happiness we had. Now it is destroyed. Danger always threatens the present. Only what is past remains unchangeable. Even if it never comes back to us, the happiness that belonged to us is still our happiness.'

His wife wrote bitterly back to him: 'Have you ever asked yourself how we manage to exist? Have you ever

seen the realities of life and wondered where your wife
and children's next meal is coming from . . . ?'

'I have no objections to this divorce,' von Schirach
wrote to the court. 'I wish her well. She is the best person
to know what she must do in this situation.'

The district youth welfare office of Kaufbeuren took
over the children's guardianship. Robert and Richard
were sent to the evangelical orphanage in Kaufbeuren,
from where, once a year, the authorities paid for a trip to
Berlin.

Today the two of them earn their own money for their
Berlin journeys. At regular intervals they write letters to
every possible authority and plead for their father's early
release. They pleaded at the Geneva and Paris conferences. Wherever the four once Allied powers are about to
sit around a conference table, Baldur von Schirach's sons
begin another campaign.

But up till now the prisoners of Spandau have not fea-
tured on any agenda at these conferences.

A Final Meeting with the Lawyer

ROBERT VON SCHIRACH, my father's interviewee, died a long time ago. He was killed in the early 1970s in a car accident. Today I sit opposite his brother in his office in the Leopoldstrasse in Munich. Klaus von Schirach is a lawyer. As we start talking, he smiles in a manner both friendly and aloof: a smile that, more than anything, intends to place a distance between us. Early on he says: 'Let me give you a tip. Write a story about the stories that have been told about us Nazi children in the media. Then you'll learn something about this society, about journalism. That would be instructive. That would be a real subject.'

Klaus von Schirach is a good-looking, elegant man, slim, with a head of thick white hair. He is wearing a violet shirt, an English checked tweed jacket, grey tie. 'You should know that we Nazi children are completely uninteresting. It's always others who read something into our lives retrospectively. There's nothing to be had from us ourselves.'

What might he mean when he says 'Then you'll learn something about this society'? Obviously he's talking about the voyeurism that surrounds it. Hey, look, there's the son of von Schirach, you know, the big Nazi's son. What do you think? Was it tough for him to have a father like that? Or maybe he turned out to be a Nazi too, like father, like son?

Or does he mean something else? The German public's reaction to the leading Nazis nowadays is to treat them a bit like animals in a zoo. A quick look at them – just long enough to make their hair stand on end – then business as usual. That way the ordinary German doesn't have to deal with his own role. Does this mean that the Nazi children have become a kind of lightning conductor for German history?

I can't ask Klaus all this in detail because our conversation takes place in an atmosphere of high tension. After a couple of minutes he's already saying: 'Well, that's that, I've already said too much about myself.' We talk a little more. He continues to tell stories that last no more than a moment, then says: 'No, I'm saying too much.' He gives the impression of a person who continually wants to pour out his heart but has told himself that that's exactly what he must never do. Maybe it is because he is suppressing so much, but as I sit opposite him I can't help thinking, This man is a whole novel.

He describes himself as having been a kind of diplomat his whole life: he has had to be one since he was a child, from the end of the war onwards. 'I've always conformed, wherever I've found myself. I've never dared do anything for myself, I've only ever wanted to make things OK for everyone else. At school I always admired the children who rebelled, the ones who were cheeky and dropped out. All I wanted was not to be noticed. Of course it had something to do with my name and my family history.' In his work as a lawyer, during divorce cases he has very often come across children like himself: the little diplomats, the ones who almost want to disappear, whose only wish is to make the smallest possible impression. Such cases are well known to psychology. Many of those who suffer in this way drop out completely or go crazy, become fighting mad, at some point in their life. 'For me it turned out all right,' says Klaus von Schirach. 'But I can't deny that my whole life has revolved around the principle of my being a crazily emotional person who, at the same time, is hyper-controlled.'

'I'm getting too private,' he suddenly says, and starts to stand up.

'Herr von Schirach,' I ask him, 'when did your mother actually die?'

'Good question,' he answers and pauses, and the silence lasts so long that one almost has to read a huge amount into it, retrospectively . . . His parents' divorce, his mother's separation from his father, hit him very hard – so others say. He never forgave his mother for not standing by his father when he was in prison, when he was a broken man.

At some point Klaus eventually says: 'In 1992, I think, yes. Some time in 1992.'

'What are the things that have marked you in your life?' I ask.

That's difficult to answer, he says. 'There were so many things.' The fact that there was no parental home, obviously. Well before the end of the war his father was not much in evidence, 'very much the same as it is for career politicians today'. When his father was released in 1966 with Albert Speer at the end of his twenty-year sentence, he was collected from prison by his three sons. But Baldur von Schirach, as Klaus says, emerged no longer on good terms with life. 'He was certainly crushed.' This was not the fault of his long prison sentence. 'As it slowly dawned on him what the results of his ideals had been, what kind of a catastrophe they had caused, from then on my father was finished.' His father had never tried to relativise the harm and the madness of National Socialism, in contrast with most other Nazi leaders, a fact of which Klaus was proud, as he had said in an earlier interview.

'What marked me?' he says again. One definite thing was a brief encounter with Hitler, says the sixty-three-year-old. It took place in Vienna, at home, and 'it was his eyes, their expression. I'll never forget it.' And Adolf Hitler generally: 'I always see this picture of him in my mind, sitting there in his armchair at his headquarters stroking his German shepherd the whole time. It's Wagner and Shakespeare and the whole thing.' He suddenly adds: 'I'm glad I had those very early experiences with National Socialism.' Glad? But it wasn't just the crimes, he says, at the beginning there were entirely different things at stake, a sense of duty, solidarity, selflessness. 'These are important.'

His father's Hitler Youths: he speaks about them as though they were his own. There were some terrific people involved. 'But they were betrayed. Just as my father was betrayed by Hitler.' After the collapse of Nazi Germany a number of these Hitler Youths had got together and paid for their leader's son's education. He keeps in touch with a number of them. 'They're good people.' Klaus von Schirach too, I understand, is living his father's life when I hear him say that they should have put the Hitler Youth at the centre of the new Germany. 'They should have made use of that energy.' They should have given them the option of allowing them to settle their own scores with the criminals, he says. The Hitler Youth. His father. The evil ones, they were the others.

Our conversation is drawing to an end. Klaus adds that National Socialism is best understood by looking at it in all aspects as a religion. The meaning of the designs, the pathos of the message: it is only by looking at it this way that one can to some extent explain why so many people followed it unconditionally.

Religion. Abuse of religion. Fundamentalism. The message was: the right of the strong. The healthy are worth more than the sick. The beautiful more than the ugly. The German more than the foreigner. The young more than the old. Strength matters, weakness deserves only scorn: it was a law of nature.

Is that perhaps what Speer's loyal colleague Theodor Hupfauer, the old Nazi, meant shortly before his death when he spoke about how comfortable he felt in the 1990s? When he sensed, as he said, that the old ideals from before were growing in value and meaning?

Is that perhaps what defines the tragedy of so many Nazi children? That what they had so badly needed in order to get on with their lives was weakness – an admission of their own weakness? Yet nothing was less vouchsafed them by their parents than that.

Klaus von Schirach sees me to the door. 'There's no doubt that it was a strange time. Twelve ridiculous years, yet they were enough to ensure that certain names would never be forgotten, and one of those names is mine. Really there's nothing more to say than that.'

Afterword

Memory is a complicated business. Everyone makes of their life their own film. What really happened? The further back the happening, the more various are the ways that question will be answered. Everyone who has experienced the laborious search for truth that goes on in any courtroom will know the problems. Forty years after its first appearance, Martin Bormann junior reread the manuscript of my father's article dating from that time, and today finds several objections to its portrayal. Some concern the time over which a number of events took place. In addition he particularly sees the description of his own path to religious belief as having been cursorily treated and containing a number of misunderstandings. We would therefore like to direct readers to the autobiography *Living Against the Shadow* (*Leben gegen den Schatten*) by Martin Bormann, in which he has extensively described his view of things and his own life's path.

All of Norbert Lebert's texts were authorised prior to publication.

The World Must Know
The History of the Holocaust as Told in the United States Holocaust Memorial Museum

by Michael Berenbaum

"A skillfully organized and clearly told account of the German Holocaust that consumed, with unparalleled malevolence, six million Jews and millions of innocent others — Protestants, Catholics, Poles, Russians, Gypsies, the handicapped, and so many others, adults and children. This important book, a vital guide through the unique corridors of the United States Holocaust Memorial Museum in Washington, D.C., merits the widest of audiences."
— Chaim Potok, author of *The Chosen* and *The Promise*

There Once Was a World
A 900-Year Chronicle of the Shtetl of Eishyshok

by Yaffa Eliach

A National Book Award Finalist

"Heartbreaking and gripping. . . . An exhaustive and kaleidoscopic history of a town whose 3,500 Jews were nearly all slaughtered."
— Stephen J. Dubner, *New York Times Book Review*

"Informative, poignant, rich with unforgettable images and memories — Yaffa Eliach's chronicle of a Jewish world that once was is a miracle in itself."
— Elie Wiesel

Available wherever books are sold

The Arms of Krupp
The Rise and Fall of the Industrial Dynasty
That Armed Germany at War

by William Manchester

"A colorful, extremely readable account. . . . To be the biographer of Krupp is to write the history of modern Germany."
— Alistair Horne, *New York Times Book Review*

"The story is irresistible. . . . It is the archetypal tale of material accumulation and growth to dehumanized power, personalized in a single family that habitually caricatured the best and worst excesses of the German character. . . . *The Arms of Krupp* has everything." — Christopher Lehmann-Haupt, *New York Times*

Double Victory
A Multicultural History of America in World War II

by Ronald Takaki

"An inspiring collection of the first-person accounts of men and women, at war and at home, who fought to make America as good as its promise." — *Washington Post Book World*

"Takaki delivers on his promise of an 'eye-level view' of the war, bringing to life the experiences and suffering of men and women whose stories have too often been overlooked in monochromatic histories of the 'good war.'" — *San Francisco Chronicle*